elsewhere, within here

World-renowned filmmaker and feminist, postcolonial thinker Trinh T. Minh-ha is one of the most powerful and articulate voices in both independent filmmaking and cultural politics.

Elsewhere, Within Here is an engaging look at travel across national borders—as a foreigner, a tourist, an immigrant, a refugee—in a pre- and post-9/11 world. Who is welcome where? What does it mean to feel out of place in the country you call home? When does the stranger appear in these times of dark metamorphoses? These are some of the issues addressed by the author as she examines the cultural meaning and complexities of travel, immigration, home and exile. The boundary, seen both as a material and immaterial event, is where endings pass into beginnings. Building upon themes present in her earlier work on hybridity and displacement in the median passage, and illuminating the ways in which "every voyage can be said to involve a re-siting of boundaries," Trinh T. Minh-ha leads her readers through an investigation of what it means to be an insider and an outsider in this "epoch of global fear."

Elsewhere, Within Here is essential reading for those interested in contemporary feminist thought and postcolonial studies.

Trinh T. Minh-ha is Professor of Rhetoric and of Gender and Women's Studies at the University of California, Berkeley. A leading feminist theorist, award-winning filmmaker, visual artist, writer, composer, cultural critic, she is the author of several influential and highly regarded books, including *When the Moon Waxes Red*, *Framer Framed*, *Cinema-Interval*, and *The Digital Film Event*, all published by Routledge

elsewhere, within here

immigration, refugeeism and the boundary event

Trinh T. Minh-ha

Routledge
Taylor & Francis Group

NEW YORK AND LONDON

First published 2011
by Routledge
270 Madison Avenue, New York, NY 10016

Simultaneously published in the UK
by Routledge
2 Park Square, Milton Park, Abingdon, Oxon OX14 4RN

Routledge is an imprint of the Taylor & Francis Group, an informa business

© 2011 Trinh T. Minh-ha Moongift Films

Typeset in Joanna and Frutiger by
Florence Production Ltd, Stoodleigh, Devon

Library of Congress Cataloging in Publication Data
A catalog record has been requested for this book

ISBN13: 978–0–415–88021–3 (hbk)
ISBN13: 978–0–415–88022–0 (pbk)
ISBN13: 978–0–203–84765–7 (ebk)

Contents

Acknowledgments

Art Work

All photos and paintings are by Jean-Paul Bourdier (www.jeanpaulbourdier.com).

Only two photos are, as indicated, stills from the digital film *Night Passage* (2004, 98 minutes) and the installation, *L'Autre marche* (2006–2009, installation along the ramp giving access to the Musée du Quai Branly, Paris, France), both by Trinh T. Minh-ha and Jean-Paul Bourdier.

Front cover and back cover: art work by Jean-Paul Bourdier, design by Alayna Johnson.

Page layout by Jean-Paul Bourdier with the assistance of Alayna Johnson.

Foreignness and the
New Color of Fear

The time now is small, mobile, portable I, light blue. In the shift from ancient territorial power to modern biopower, virtual boundlessness in globalization is widely praised as the overcoming of frontiers. The globe is evoked in terms of both a closely knit village, and a new, dishomogenous metropolis. Yet, the talk on the world political page is all about closing down, curtailing movements, reinforcing borders, building new fences, installing more checkpoints, fortifying security zones, setting up gated communities, and worse, sealing an entire nation into restricted areas. *Says a voice from cyberspace: "Call it a fence built to 'make good neighbors' but it is still a wall, and remember what the Berlin Wall was called on the other side; it was an Anti-Fascist Protection Barrier."* Stop. Close up and exclude. But moreover, divide, subjectify, and control. While binding, blind, shut off and wall in.

The epoch of global fear has provoked extreme reactions and sentenced the world to indefinite confinement behind the bars of homeland security. With the political backlash against marked foreigners, foreign-born or foreign-looking members, asylum and refugeeism remain a key political issue, while immigration and (dis)integration, arbitrarily connected to terrorism, have become an explosive matter of voting debate in national politics. Everywhere, migration has shot up the list of governmental concerns. Questions arising on the move, at the borders, in the encounter with the other, and when stranger meets stranger, all tend to intensify around the problem of the *other* foreigner—someone doubly strange, who doesn't *speak* or look like the rest of us, being paradoxically at once exotic guest and abhorred enemy.

> This is her home
> this thin edge of
> barbwire
> —Gloria Anzaldúa

Story of the Wall

Until then . . . Many stories of the wall have been told. Master musician Hazrat Inayat Khan tells, for example, of an ancient story on the wall of mystery in the East. As far as memory could recall, whoever is tempted to climb up the wall to look at what lies on the other side, ends up happily jumping over it, never to look back again. *Until then*

. . . wanting to have the cake and eat it all, the people left behind scheme on. They've got to know without having to go, for fear of losing the view they've gained on this side. *Until*. Finally, the day comes when they decide to catch a climber in his act, putting chains on his feet so as to prevent him from going over. As soon as the climber sees the other side and smiles in delight, those safely posted at the foot of the wall swiftly pull him back, showering him with questions only to find out to their great disappointment that he has lost his speech.

What the mind sees, it tells with words, so goes a saying. The world one knows is the world one sees around oneself—whose limited and hierarchized access is protected with ever-higher and mightier walls. What lies beyond is often thought of as all fable. And although living in two dualistic worlds (here versus there) proves to be still acceptable to the rational mind, living in two and many non-opposing worlds—all located in the very same place as where one is—inevitably inscribes silence. Not from elsewhere, but more specifically, from an elsewhere within here. Whatever happens at the moment of visual encounter has induced a state of muteness. If those who stay tend to meet such an inability to speak with great disappointment—as a loss, a lack to be filled, a deficiency in need of rehabilitation and (re) integration—those who leave and risk in multiplicity, often tend to go on cold for a while, living life as it comes, fasting verbally and linguistically, before learning how to speak again, anew.

. *Speaking frees thought from the optical imperative that in the Western tradition, for thousand of years, has subjugated our approach to things, and induced us to think under the guaranty of light or under the threat of its absence.*
—Maurice Blanchot

What lies on the far side is often thought of as old wives' fable . . . until one by one, the specter of the disappeared-beyond-the-wall—those who embark, willingly, unwillingly, on a journey of no return—come back silently to haunt those who stay. Expectations for stories of stranger-than-fiction realities meet with a mute wall of separation. On the one hand, seeing is seeing only what is containable in words, and speaking is speaking only as dictated by the readily visible. On the other, with no qualifying adjectives and adverbs, speaking is not seeing, and *seeing is: not speaking*. The first is heard as a simple negative: thinking, speaking, writing cannot be reduced to the measure of the eye. While the second is sounded both ways, as a negative-affirmative: the two activities are at once distinct and interchangeable (but not same) in their multiplicity—the eye hears, the ear sees. In deciding to stay or to leave, turning away from the all too speakable, is not necessarily turning back round toward the unspeakable or the inexpressible. When One is one with many (no tenable binary), the question is not so much to choose between sight and speech, as *to see what the eye hears, and hear what the ear sees*.

This story of the wall was primarily told as a story of music. *The deeper one's understanding of life, the more music one can listen to* (Inayat Khan).[1] Alive, certain walls rise as hymn, voice, and rhythm across centuries and histories. Each, singular in its tonality. Each, potentially drawing attention to a blinding blockage of one's making; a protective impediment that feeds one's desires and fears, and compels one to stare at—rather than gaze beyond— what obstructs one's horizons until it *disappears*. The impasse turns out to be a passage, and a creatively dangerous passageway. Indeed, what is there in music that attracts all those who listen to it? What's so alluring in a wall that inevitably drives people to breaching and surmounting it? No matter how impenetrable it promises to be with its sophisticated system of remote surveillance, as soon as those on one side put it up, those on the other side are propelled to risk their lives crossing over and under it.

You close down, we walk around. You erect, we dig. You dig, we dig and dig further. Bind and soon, you'll be tearing madly at the wall, and the bonds you've created. What you want to hear, you hear not. For, what finds its way out from the underground and the out there is spoken in rhythms and tones, in a language that solicits a different hearing. Trying to listen to it is to give ear to the ties that bind the hearing deaf and the speaking mute. But with what ear does one receive the other side of speech? Already there, never gone. Neither out-side nor in-side, the music of alterity has been playing on without interruption—if only one can hear it. Sight, crossing over, is not merely sight, but speech freed from the limitations of speech. As the voice of ancient Asian wisdom often said, what one is not ready for, one will have no ear. And when one is ready, there's no speaker to be found.

The Wall Event

The wall, in its wide range of material and figural manifestations, remains actively ambivalent in its transgressive and regressive presence. At first, it all seems as if everything depends on which side of the wall one finds oneself. But, as border inhabitants acutely remark, *the high wall that keeps out is the same wall that keeps in.* Outside and inside: again the pair hardly functions as a binary, despite the authorities' colossal effort to censor and separate. What offers itself as a hymn or a song, also stands as a sign of isolation and fear, a scar in the environmental landscape, a visual statement of one's relationship with one's neighboring communities across the region.

The wall of security is in fact a wall of insecurity. At the U.S.–Mexico borders, primary barriers of different kinds are doubled and tripled as massive secondary and tertiary barriers with "climb proof" top are added to create further obstacles. *"A border wall tells the world we are a fearful nation,"* says another voice from cyberspace. Concerned citizens who oppose "these ill-conceived walls founded in current notions of racism," have insisted on how inadequate an answer to the problem of illegal immigration a wall by itself proves to be: "You show me a 50-foot wall, and I'll show you a 51-foot ladder." Even Border Patrol agents are skeptical and unimpressed with the continuing call to seal the frontier with high technology. They consider the "virtual fence" project to be a "colossal waste of money" and complain about expensive, elaborate border technology as "yielding few apprehensions," while "resulting in needless investigations of legitimate activity." Those determined to cross excel at figuring out ways around the technological sentries, often breaching the barriers in broad daylight. *Muros de odio,* as it is called in the U.S. southern borderlands, the border wall is the symbol of a new hatred which America is known to have effectively fueled.

Elsewhere, as in Iraq for example, the three-mile concrete wall, built in Baghdad with American support and guidance to isolate the Sunni neighborhood of Adhamiya from surrounding Shiite areas, had also drawn intense criticism from its residents. As the media reported, angered and "united in their contempt" for the imposing structure, both Sunni and Shiites in the affected neighborhood remain incredulous as to the "inhumane manner" with which they were "transformed into caged animals," and shut off from other parts of Baghdad. The Gate Community concept was used as a tactic to "break the cycle of sectarian violence," but as the residents astutely remarked, erecting concrete walls between neighborhoods was clearly a sign of rather than a solution to the collapse in security. Many viewed the "the sectarian wall" as yet another too-little-too-late attempt by the Occupiers to find a temporary solution at the expense of the Iraqis. While the soldiers jokingly called it, "The Great Wall of Adhamiya," some political analysts referred to it as "The Great Wall of Segregation."

The number of walls, which increased day after day, suffocating the people and turning Baghdad into a city of barriers, had also led people to resort to imaginative counter-measures. In response to the Occupier's strangely undemocratic measures of safety, barren blast walls thus became "oases of art," prompting, for example, a group of artists, named Jidar or "Wall," at first to paint them in a single light blue, thereby opening up the view so as to sky gaze there where it has been shut off; then, to come up with elaborate murals depicting ancient historical scenes, as in the area near the Baghdad Hotel. Painting the walls may make the artists "feel less helpless," but one wonders what it initially takes for the creative mind to smile and sing as it does (rather than yell out in anger and distress as with wall graffiti around the world, for example), when it sees in these miles of deadly barriers a sweeping *open canvas* . . .

> *The wall that was dismantled in Berlin is being re-built brick by brick . . . The ideology might be different, but the desperation for dominance was the same.*
> —Wole Soyinka

In fear, a wall often reminds one of another wall. Many Iraqis inevitably found a parallel with Israel's network of barriers and checkpoints, as they often evoked the similarity in suppressing violence, between what Americans did in Iraq and what Israelis were doing in the West Bank. The issue of border crossings is one of the most intractable, and outside of Iraq, the highly controversial Israeli West-Bank wall undergoes yet further comparisons. Its erection is widely seen as a concrete expression of the bantustanization of the Palestinian areas, dividing strategically the land, quarantining the Palestinian people in "bantustans," or ghettos à la South Africa, disconnecting them from international borders, creating new bizarre boundaries on top of old ones, and subjecting them to a grotesque regime of gates and permits (such as driving them into situations where they are compelled to enter the city illegally so as to obtain a permit enabling them to enter it legally).

"*Fourteen years of negotiations have brought us nothing but a wall,*" said a Fatah leader in Ramallah. The Wall here is said to be "a monument to the failure of the peace process." It is not so much about the wall as about the disappearing of a people—out of sight, off records; about land, water, and the unmaking of Palestine—"a structural negation of the right to food, as it will effectively forestall forever the possibility of a viable Palestinian state" (Jean Ziegler, the United Nations Special Rapporteur on the Right to Food).[2] Israelis most commonly know it as the "security fence," "anti-terrorist fence," or "separation fence;" while Palestinians call it the "racial segregation wall." Equally telling is the English name referred to by its opponents: the "Apartheid Wall."

The Call of the Tricolor Flag

Democracy remains an everyday fight and a constant act of border crossing. At a time when the rhetoric of blurred boundaries and of boundless access is at its most impressive flourish, the most regressive walls of separation and racial discrimination, of hatred and fear, of humiliation and powerlessness continue to be erected around the world to divide and conquer, exacerbating existing conflicts as one world, one nation, one community, one group continue to be dramatically raised against another. For those on which the wall is imposed, the response has been almost unanimously defiant across contexts and countries. "It's an insult. We'll make tunnels." Or: "let them build their wall, and it will be breached with impunity." Again, the issue of having a wall built is not about the wall, but about putting to use, in the guise of security, a network of what is thought to be the most efficient mechanisms of strangulation, humiliation and domination.

While the era of colonization has been officially proclaimed to have practically reached an end, invasion, occupation, disruption and relocation—in other words, colonization by other means—continue to set the stage for unending aggression and destruction. A state of urgency has become the routine. In the United States, September Eleven has dramatically changed the stakes for those caught in the deep tangle of immigration laws. As immigration reform falters, the focus obsessively returns to militarization of the border and to advances of civil and military technologies that either have no interest in democracy or make a fool of it. Success in border battles is being measured in proportion to the gain in violence: in Border Patrol theory, the deadlier the immigrants' fight, the more control the patrolling side is said to gain.

In the quasi-neurotic state of self-inducing fear, every immigrant or voyager of color is a potential terrorist. Racial and national profiling at airport security has been well documented. Each time a new harrowing plot to blow up one or a series of passenger jets is foiled, new security holes are exposed and new measures are added to those already in place. Instead of fading away, the bans issued by the Transportation Security Administration take roots and become a means of posturing power at every level of security activities. Officials have been encouraging people to look out and report on individuals whose movements they deem "suspect," and stories around many of these inevitably grotesque reports abound in the media. Those targeted or "randomly selected" for security checks are not only those whose political background poses a threat to the ruling authorities, but most often those in possession of a "Muslim name," and those who simply "look" other, queer, or shady to the "normal" eye.

Every official triumph in the struggle against terrorism is spiked with a heavier dose of anxiety. We're warned again and again against false comfort, and we're made to feel we're not safe *yet*. Never quite safe, for the world we knew before September Eleven no longer existed, or so it was repeatedly said. In the aftermath of the attack, the American flag as a sign of patriotism and nationalism gained such an appeal that people of all walks of life felt the need to display it, not only by carrying it but also by embodying it, painting it directly on their skin or wearing it publicly on their clothing, scarves, lapel pins and hair bands. One of the most poignant and memorable moments was when, a few days after the fall of the Twin Towers, the media recorded the whooping call of the Star-Spangled Banner: in the flurry of flag displays, amidst tremor and trepidation, one suddenly catches a glimpse of the underlying divide that surreptitiously surfaced as the patriotic fervor swept across the country. With images dominating the news, of White America affirming itself to be the real religion of the country, one was also shown images in the margins, of smiling "Arab-looking minorities," who hastened to cover their stores and business places with flags of all sizes, so as to publicly display their allegiance to the United States.

Members of the Afghan or Arab Muslim communities who shared their stories online and spoke among friends, related how out of fear, people around them rushed out to buy the American flag to avoid accusations of being "Un-American." Experiencing a harsh backlash of public perception, they earnestly put the flag up outside their houses and their places of worship, as well as on the windows and bumpers of their cars. Thus, collectively made to bear the burden of representation like other marginalized communities, they went out of their way doing things deemed "American" in order to (re) gain acceptance. The more immigrants in an area, the more homes decorated with flags. In their need for an ostensible sign of belonging, the flag became a way for self-protection against the wrath of the racially privileged. A member of the Sikh American community (Manjit Singh) recalled the case of his friend from New York who went to India and brought back four thousand turbans in the red, blue and white colors of the American Flag. Intent upon distributing them out, the friend wondered aloud whether he should ask Sikh Americans to participate in the July 4th parade with these tricolor turbans on their heads . . .

An infamous line much quoted from president George W. Bush's address to Congress on September 20, 2001 reads: "Either you are with us, or you are with the terrorists." For many Arab Americans, the lesson of September Eleven was a racial lesson. Never believing it could happen to them, those who, before the Event, easily dismissed, if not looked down on, all matters pertaining to racial discrimination, had a hard time accepting their eviction from Whiteness. As writer and activist Carol Chehade noted, "The backlash we're now receiving is from the same whip we've borrowed to lash out against African Americans . . . Many in my Arab American community are surprised when they are treated un-White . . . Our disassociation [from Black people] would not be so evident if we weren't ruthlessly trying to move up the racial hierarchy so that we can be closer to Whiteness . . . Being a 'minority' has less to do with what we look like and more to do with how we think."[3]

In the flag's proud symbol of unity ("United We Stand") lies a dividing marker: on one side of the banner: the Old Glory, strength, courage, patriotism. On the other side: intimidation, exclusion, censorship, jingoism, vengeance and war. The stain of racism has not gone away. W. E. B. Du Bois' remark, "the problem of the Twentieth Century is the problem of the color line," seems to have taken on a new lease of life, with a new hue and tonality. Times of disaster bring about a sharp awareness of reality, as it is: fragile—externally, but more so, internally. With the fall of the Twin Towers, a symbol of double invincibility and almightiness has powerfully shifted to that of a disappearance of plenipotence itself. Nothing seems solid and with the subsequent economic downturn, what appears ordinarily plain solid—the house, or the walls we build step by step for our families and toil to preserve during our lifetime—suddenly show their friability.

Thanks to the anonymity of a remote-control aggressiveness and counter-aggressiveness, opacity—the opacity of solid matter—seems no more than a mere temporary obstacle to overcome. The incessantly fortified line dividing here from there may turn out in the end to be an "optical illusion." Always lurking are the cracks and fissures whose invisibility may at any time turn visible with a dice of destiny. Consciousness becoming attuned to reversible endings and beginnings, remembers this other line by President Harry S. Truman, when in 1959, he denounced the House Un-American Activities Committee (which investigated, among others, the activities of Communists in the United States) as the "most un-American thing in the country today."

I

home

The Traveling Source

Far Away, From Home
(The Comma Between)

A shortened version was first published in *Eyewitness to History/Augenzeugen der Geschichte*, ed. Weltenburger e.V. in English and in German, trans. Madeleine Bernstorff (Hanover, Germany: Weltenburger e.V., 2001), pp. 86–129.

When I first came to the United States from Vietnam in 1970, for several months I could not get a good sleep during the night. No matter how hard I tried to surrender to it, I repeatedly found myself lying still, eyes wide open in the dark, waiting. Waiting for what? Waiting, I thought, for dawn, so that I could finally fall asleep a few hours before starting my morning activities. During the daytime, sleep would often take me by surprise, and in between tasks I would catch myself napping, with remorse. But when night fell, and it was clearly time to rest and rightfully claim my due from the day of work, I again felt strangely uneasy. As the sounds of the world outside faded away, the night suddenly took on a threatening presence. Rather than finding peace and repose in the warmth of the bed, I was dreading what to me seemed like an endless moment of false cessation. So I waited, unable to figure out my uneasiness, until one night a distant shooting in the streets outside unexpectedly shed a light on the situation. I realized I was briefly home again.

Sleepless Silence

What appeared most strikingly foreign to me then were these long, spacious American nights enveloped by uninterrupted silence. It was in this kind of silence that I experienced the keen feeling of being different—a stranger living in a strange land. The "normal" land at the time was a war-torn land, whose daily sound environment populated by the war machines did not simply stop after dark. Its rarefaction at night made it all the more terrifying, as it tended to take one by surprise during sleep time when one was at one's most vulnerable. As the saying goes, "The enemy attacks by night." This held true for people on both sides of the old north–south divide in Vietnam, but in the southern territories where I was then—I was born in Hanoi and grew up in Saigon—

the situation was particularly intense, for example, in 1968 and in the years after. The South faced intensive fighting, marked by the Tet Offensive, which saw a massive attack by Communist forces catch the city and its densely populated environs by surprise on New Year's Eve.

It was the time when we were surviving on plain rice and water, with 24-hour curfews, often with no electricity, nothing to barter for food and barely any sleep. As our house was located next to the national police quarter, we were inevitably living in *wait* for heavy, unpredictable mortar and rocket fire attacks, spending endless nights packed together in between sandbags in our small bathroom. Steep silence then usually signaled the imminence of an explosion. Whenever it appeared, the heart pounded in recognition, and we would stop dead in our activities—in the midst of conversation and even of quiet thinking. The whole body was an ear, and my ear, trained to the sounds of war, was always on the alert for that split second of silence before the blast of rockets, which would be followed by the crackle of small-arm fire or the wail of sirens and the shouts and cries of afflicted witnesses. That ear needed some time to adjust to the sounds and silences of peace.

Today, when I'm asked where home is for me, I am struck by how far away it is; and yet, home is nowhere else but right here, at the edge of this body of mine. Their land is my land, their country is my country. The source has been traveling and dwelling on hybrid ground. Home and abroad are sometimes intuitively determined according to the light of the sky on location, other times by the taste of native water, or by the smell of the environment, and other times yet, by the nature of the surrounding silence. Home then is not only in the eye, the tongue and the nose, but it is also, as in my case, acutely in the ear. It is said, for example, that writers or the diverse Diasporas around the world live in a double exile: away from their native land and away from their mother tongue. Displacement takes on many faces and is our very everyday dwelling. (But to say this is hardly to say anything foreign to this age of new technology where, with the spread of wireless devices, people of the mobile world spend their time more in airports, airplanes and in their cars than at home.)

Seven years after this first encounter with the American nighttime soundscape, I was to live the experience again, albeit very differently, in Senegal, where I lived and taught for three years at the National Conservatory of Music of Dakar while doing field research across West African countries. The experience of Africa was a catalyst in my own journey. There are many aspects of African cultures for which I felt deep affinities—including the legacies of French colonization, which both Vietnam and Senegal had undergone. But the one dimension of the culture that profoundly struck me during my first year there was again the language of silence. In other words, silence not as opposed to language, but as a choice not to verbalize, a will not to say, a necessary interval in an interaction—in brief, as a means of communication of its own. With many years spent in the States before going to Africa, I had almost forgotten and given up the importance of the role of silence in Asian communicative contexts, and had come to accept that silence could not be communicated unless it was a collective, timely produced silence. To my great delight and surprise, however, people there knew how to listen to my silences in all complexities and subtleties, and I learned that this mute language could be effectively shared. *In their silences, I returned home.*

Having lived, taught and done extensive work in more than one culture—Vietnamese, French, American, African and more recently, Japanese—I have always resisted the comfort of conventional categories. And my works are all sustained attempts to shift set boundaries—whether cultural, political or artistic. Even today, after two decades of relentless critical work on the politics of racially, sexually and professionally discriminatory practices, it still happens that when I'm invited to speak, I'm asked with great expectations to speak as a representative—of a culture, a people, a country, an ethnicity or a gender considered to be mine and my own. In other words, tell us about Vietnam, be woman, talk Asian, stay within the Third World. We all seem to know the dilemma of speaking within authorized boundaries, and yet the urge to orientalize the Oriental and to africanize the African continues to lurk behind many Westerners' well-intended attempts to promote better understanding of cultural difference.

This tendency to commodify diversity for faster consumption has at times thrown me into great distress, and for a long while, at least in the United States, whenever friendly editors of journals and anthologies asked me to contribute writing in the areas of race, ethnicity, class, gender and postcolonial theories, the only work I sent out for publication was poetry. Some academics and orthodox Marxists squirmed at the idea of publishing what to their eyes were only "love poems;" others accepted them willy-nilly; but others yet were simply elated. Besides constituting a no-more-of-the-same tactics on my part, such a gesture is also a way of signaling a different practice of poetry, the opposition of which is certainly not prose—for the poetic lies first and foremost in the ear that hears language—and the world—in its music and intervals.

Thanks to this ear, the one satisfactory way of dealing with this problem is to place it in the wider context of our troubled world. What, indeed, makes us endlessly return to the sources—those ancient, unknowable sources that keep inquiries alive and challenge every boundary set up for strategic or survival purposes? Where do we come from? Where do we go? What keeps us holding on to the thread of life, doing what we each do so earnestly in our daily existence? And what ear has suddenly caught on the whence and whither of life?

The Tea and the Tear

Vietnam, a small country, a very big name; an exceptionally famed nation and yet a very little-known culture. Despite the new appeal of Vietnam, due to its more recent opening and its history of resistance, its people and their rich cultural legacies remain largely invisible. After decades of existing only through the horrors of war as electronically projected into TV owners' living rooms, Vietnam since the 1990s has been attracting a new wave of Western onlookers: veterans trying to heal in reconnecting with their past interactions with Vietnam and troops of tourists in search of the Indochine nostalgically portrayed in more recent mainstream films—lavishly set up and retouched with its colonial buildings, with its ethereal islands and lagoons and its melancholic sense of loss. The Vietnam fever overseas has been steadily on the rise the last two decades. Tourism is certainly one of Vietnam's burgeoning industries and during the year 2000, some 1.8 million tourists were reported to have poured into the country. Images of Vietnam's peaceful countryside, with its radiantly green rice paddies and its powder-soft sand beaches, widely serve as a marketing tool for the film and tourist industries. Even the famous Cu Chi tunnels from which surprise attacks were launched against U.S. forces are now routinely part of the war-theme tour sites. With no resentment, local people happily oblige.

Many years ago I wrote that as a name, Vietnam was constantly evoked as an exemplary model of revolution: She was "a nostalgic cult object for those who, while admiring unconditionally the revolution, do not seem to take any genuine, sustained interest in the troubled reality of Vietnam in her social and cultural autonomy . . . The longer Vietnam is extolled as the unequal model of the struggle against Imperialism, the more convenient it is for the rest of the world to close their eyes on the harrowing difficulties the nation, governed by a large post-revolutionary bureaucracy, continues to face in trying to cope with the challenge of recovery."[1] Today, things have changed for the better as Vietnam continues to attract new generations of visitors eager to see the country in a new light, and the government is quick to declare that Vietnam has become more than a name, "not just a war, but a country." However, if Vietnam is definitely on display in many Western media and art exhibition venues, the vogue now is exclusively the rural idyll, the media-created untouched countryside or else the exotic stylish urban chic of Saigonese (local people have not quite gotten used to calling it Ho Chi Minh City), which provide the perfect contrast to the bloody, also media-created, dehumanizing images of Vietnam in the sixties and early seventies. As long as visitors indulge in "Namstalgia," everything is under control, for people can be distracted from the harsh realities of the government's rule and the political tensions that afflict the country.

To share something of Vietnamese culture, let me relate a story I've often heard during my childhood—a well-known Vietnamese tale named after its two protagonists, *Truong Chi, My Nuong*. As with all tales, its content varies slightly with each storyteller, depending on where the teller sees the enchantment, the struggle and the moral in the story. In its translations, the tale has been given such titles as, "The Love Crystal" (by Pham Duy Khiem) or "Story of the Spellbinding Voice" (by Nguyen Xuan Hung) or as I myself would also like to call it, "The Tea and the Tear."

The tale sketches the profile of a maiden (My Nuong) who, as the daughter of a powerful mandarin, grows up in seclusion behind the high walls of her father's palace. She spends her time practicing arts deemed suitable to her rank and gender—such as embroidery, poetry and painting—and she sees the world outside as framed by the window of her room. The daily view that sustains her melancholic daydreaming is that of the river flowing below the palace and the reflections of the landscape in the water.

One drizzly afternoon, however, she is drawn to the window by the sound of a deep, melodious song that rises from the river. There she sees, gliding on the water, a boat and a fisherman pulling on his net whom she can hear singing, but whose features she cannot distinguish from afar. Day after day, she listens to the voice that comes to her in her solitude. One can't really tell how and what exactly in the song, the music and the voice has made its way into her budding heart, but the story goes that on the day the voice suddenly stops, she catches herself waiting until late in the evening. Vainly she continues thereafter to wait for it at her window every afternoon, but nowhere is the familiar silhouette of the fisherman and his boat to be seen. She goes on waiting until she falls severely ill. As she lets herself be wasted away, the best doctors are summoned, but none is able to determine the cause of her suffering. Her parents become more and more alarmed at her inexplicable illness, when suddenly she recovers. The voice has returned.

Informed by a servant, the father has the fisherman (Truong Chi) brought to his palace to sing in a room next to his daughter's. Upon her request, however, the mandarin agrees to let her see the man in person. Did he not know then where such a fatherly consent would lead? For, from the very first look, something unavoidably ends in the maiden's heart. The voice loses its charm and the spell is lifted. Some tellers would expand here on the repelling ugliness of the man, stressing the contrast between his fairy voice and his burnt, withered and deformed physical attributes caused by hard work outdoors. In any case, the young woman was said to be definitively cured of her illness, and soon, forgetting what fed her dreams, she returns to a normal life.

As for the poor fisherman who until then remains innocent of his music's power, it is his turn to receive the fatal blow at the sight of the maiden's appearance. He catches the sickness and, consumed by a love without hope, he pines away in silence. The man perishes in solitude, keeping the secret sealed with his death. Buried, his remains are exhumed a year after by his family, so they can be transferred to a final resting place. What they find then amidst the skeletal remains is an unusually translucent stone in place of his heart, which they faithfully hang, in his memory, on the bow of his boat.

One day, as the mandarin is crossing the river, he sees with admiration the stone at the front of the boat shuttling between the two shores. He buys it and asks a jeweler to fashion it into a teacup. As things turns out, however, every time tea is poured into the cup, the image of a fisherman moving slowly around with his boat appears. The mandarin's daughter learns of the miracle and wants to see it for herself. She pours tea into the cup and the fisherman's image appears. Remembering, she cries. A teardrop falls on the cup and the latter disappears, dissolving into water.

So ends the tale of *Truong Chi, My Nuong.*

The Debt of Love

A story is told to invite talk around it. One can take it as a shallow piece of entertainment; or one can receive it as a profound gift traveling from teller to teller, handed down from generation to generation, repeatedly evoked in its moral truth and yet never depleted in its ability to instruct, to delight and to move. For me, this tale functions at least on three levels: as a cultural marker, a political pointer and an artistic quest. While remaining very specific to Vietnamese culture in its concerns and colorings, it can easily fare across cultural borders and struggles. One is reminded here of such classics in the West as, for example, Beauty and the Beast, Orpheus and Eurydice, or Ulysses and the Sirens— to mention just a few.

With the creative works of the disfranchised and of political prisoners around the world in mind, one can say that just as poetry cannot be reduced to being a mere art for the rich and idle, storytelling is not a luxury or a harmless pastime. It is, indeed, in the tale that one is said to encounter the genius of a people. Tales are collective

dreams that move and mold societies, revealing the actual fears, desires, aims and values by which communities are shaped. In Vietnam (like in other cultures), although some ancient tales are dotted here and there with details that speak of their hybrid origins— from India, Champa and China, for example—as an element of civilization thoroughly adapted to rural life, these tales remain loyal to the sensibility and the wisdom of the local people. No book, no substantial study on the history, culture and civilization of Vietnam written by Vietnamese can do without the body of tales, which constitute the core of a popular literature widely spread among all classes of its society.

The tales not only condense certain characteristics of the everyday person and the people's customs, they often also deal with complex social relations; with the fate of an individual; or else, with the faithful love between a worker figure (like a woodcutter, a fisherman, a hard-working mother or a Cinderella-type orphan) and a noble (like a princess, a lord or a scholar). They tell of the latent antagonisms between rich and poor in the heart of rural communities whose tranquil and timeless setting can be very deceptive. As with stories among oppressed and disfranchised groups around the world, the Vietnamese tale allows its tellers to allude to issues of poverty, social injustice and class conflict.

Tales often read like profound strategies of survival. In them, divergence and inequality, if not conflict, are often set within the framework of a patriarchal economy. The human condition and its dilemmas are featured in the fate of an individual who is likely to be poor, unfortunate, rejected or plainly stupid, but whose honesty and goodness usually lead to a rewarding ending. The world seems, at first sight, to be simplified into two categories of people: those whose power derives from material advantages and those whose force belongs to a different order—one that exceeds ordinary sight and is commonly termed "magical," "shamanistic," "supernatural," "mystical," or merely "superstitious." This division, which dates back to the night of time, continues to prevail today, and it takes us little to see in these two kinds of people a proliferation of dualities, such as the divisions between North and South, the West and the Rest, conqueror and native, colonizer and colonized, state and non-state, science and art, culture and nature, materiality and spirituality, masculine and feminine, or more intimately, between inside and outside, self and other.

Hope is, however, always kept alive in the tale—hope, and not expectation, for it is through fairies, deities, and genies, or as in the case of the tale told earlier, through the forces that exceed the lifetime of an individual, that people who knew the lore of survival seek to solve difficult situations and social inequity. As Native American storytellers remind us, stories are what we have to fight off illness and death, they make medicines and are a healing art. Bringing the impossible within reach and making us realize with poignancy that *material reality is only one dimension of reality*, tales address our longing of a more equitable world built on our struggle as well as on our dreams, our aspirations and actions for peace. Needless to say, there are many other tales that are just as relevant, if not more adequate, for a discussion on Vietnamese culture and politics; especially those in which historical and mythical elements are tightly woven and the opposition between oppressors and victims more directly politicized. However, I would rather choose this tale of Tea and Tear, precisely because it is not a story of black and white, or of war and conflict, but a story of love.

By making such a choice, I am perhaps only following an old path, for the most famous work of Vietnamese literature, and the most widely remembered national poem of Vietnam is not an epic poem, but a love poem: *The Tale of Kieu*, written in the early nineteenth century, whose 3,254 verses are known by heart to all classes of people in Vietnam and cherished even among those who are illiterate. Today the younger generations of the Vietnamese Diaspora in the United States and in Europe invoke it as one of the very few treasures of their culture, which they wish to preserve. I myself have taken inspiration from it in two of my films, *Surname Viet Given Name Nam* and *A Tale of Love*. The image of *Kieu* as a sacrificial woman in tears and as a model of feminine loyalty has been appropriated and accordingly adapted to innumerable official and non-official contexts. It stands both as a denunciation of corrupt feudalism and American imperialism, and as an allegory of the tragic fate of Vietnam under colonialism or else of the boat people whose silent exodus went on well after the war ended in 1975—to the embarrassment of the international community.

Why does such a patriarchal society like Vietnam identify the destiny of its country with the fate and deeds of a woman like Kieu? Perhaps, because Kieu is not merely Kieu to our eyes. We easily forget the woman in all women, and although Kieu personifies love, what many of us perceive through her, understandably enough, are the male author, Nguyen Du (1765–1820), and the questing of his official life. By an astute shift of gender, he lives on with the tale, lamenting the promiscuous political affiliations of his time. His own dilemma was that of having to survive the Tay-son revolution and to serve the Nguyen dynasty, while remaining in his heart faultlessly loyal to the Le dynasty (1427–1788), which the Tay-son had destroyed. Perhaps it's also because Kieu's passion-driven life is marked, despite her extreme beauty, sacrifice, and loyalty, by unremitting misfortunes: for her family's survival, she is forced to undergo intolerable injustices and to prostitute herself, thereby breaking her vows to her first love. Or perhaps it's because through Kieu's story, the worst imaginable and the very best of that which has been called "human" is vividly brought into the picture. And then perhaps, as it is widely perceived, it's because this unpredictable turn in her life (in one's life—as war victim, refugee, exile, émigré, prisoner of conscience, homeless, mourner, etc.) results both from social injustices and from an old debt that one carries on from one's previous lives. This is where the tale strikes a most sensitive chord in the Vietnamese psyche.

Man of Tea

As I was often told in my childhood, by relatives and teachers, the much coveted land of Vietnam, marked by natural disasters, internal turbulence and foreign domination is not a gift that has fallen from the sky. For over four thousand years, our people have had to earn it with sweat and tears, acre by acre, carrying on a multiple struggle against the forces of nature—floods, droughts, typhoons year in year out for millennia—against civil conflicts and against foreign aggression. The country has long been the theater of wars and destructions: ten centuries of direct Chinese domination, from 111 BC to the tenth century; then, indirect domination until the end of the nineteenth century, followed by French occupation from the end of the nineteenth century to 1954; Japanese occupation alongside a French colonial administration from 1940 to 1945; and twenty years of

American involvement until 1975. The floods recurring in Vietnam have devastated many provinces in the South, wrecking at times half a million homes and affecting nearly three million people. Vietnam's unending suffering has been often related in terms of an ancient debt that she has not yet succeeded in paying off, even as of today, when one considers how poisoned her landscape has also come to be with the hellish legacy of Agent Orange and the millions of land mines scattered about the provinces, ready to go off.

In our tale of *The Love Crystal*, every detail seems to speak volumes for the debt it owes to a culture that has taken so much inspiration from the Chinese and yet has been resisting this so fiercely as to fall into the trap of defining its identity mainly in counteraction to everything thought to be Chinese. This love–hate relationship shows through the evocation of the mandarinate system of ruling which Vietnam had inherited from China. The fisherman's love-at-first-sight is kept secret even as it leads to his death because as much as the created class gap makes it impossible for him to realize his dream in his lifetime, it also betrays the hidden aspiration of the disenfranchised to reach the status of the enfranchiser. And the mandarin's daughter, who awakens to love at the sound of his song is unreachable, for she is not of this world—or of the world of the manual labor class. Details such as the high walls of the palace that separate them and the fashioning of the poor man's heart into a teacup to gratify the aesthetic demand of the leisure class all seem at first to converge to emphasize the impossibility of their union.

The same may be said of the gender divide. The benevolence of the father figure only serves to naturalize better the sorry condition of women in the past and the present male-dominated society of Vietnam. Striking similarities can be drawn between the tale of *The Love Crystal* and the well-known contemporary novel *The Crystal Messenger* (1988) by Pham Thi Hoai, one of the two women in a small group of post-war writers that emerged in Vietnam in the late 1980s. Eloquent and cleverly evasive, these writers' works dare to depart from the stifling, controlled world of official narratives to offer fresh views of Vietnamese society. Hoai's novel manages, for example, through wit, humor and oblique imagery, to denounce family, Party and state in their officialized corruptions, ignorance and incompetence. Its narration presents a scathing commentary on modern society through the eyes of a woman not only trapped in the dwarf body of a young girl—she stopped growing up at the age of fourteen—but also trapped in the sixteen-square-meter room that constitutes the whole of her dwelling space. A woman's place is well defined, and as practices around the world show, despotic boundaries do not necessarily need to be material. Thus, it is through the magic rectangle of her window that the woman in the novel spends her time filtering the world outside, which she radically divides into two: that of *homo-A*, those who know how to love, and that of *homo-Z*, those who don't. Such a reduction of place, of mankind and, as she affirms, of her own body is not fortuitous; it is the fruit of many years of mental and physical exertion.

The author of this remarkable novel now lives in Germany. She, like the character of her novel, seems to abhor everything that smacks of romanticism, and yet it is worth noting that what lies at the core of the novel's worldview is *love*. And this radically modern view owes its lifeblood, whether consciously or not, to the body of Vietnamese folktales of which *The Love Crystal* is only an example. *The deeper and wider you go, the older the story.* Here one also touches on the heart of the tale itself: that which we are all bound to face at the end of our journey—the debt of love or, simply, the Debt. Thanks to it, what is made unreachable through the divides of class and gender finds its own way out. Waiting in loyalty to the call of one's heart is what it takes to "win over" an impossible situation. In time, the dark secret of the fisherman, his buried love and fidelity have crystallized to become the primal material for the creation of a refined object of pleasure—an object whose unusual function is to hold both the tea and the image it persistently produces.

Image, man and cup all disappear with the contact of a single teardrop. As her heart melts, his crystallized heart dissolves. The irruption of the Debt into visibility, the resurrection of the man's appearance in the tea is followed by its return to water, to formlessness and to invisibility. Weeping relieves; the pair of love and loss that runs through the story in the dark light of suffering returns at the end of the tale, transformed and freed by the two waters: tea and tear. Tea as it is well known in Asia, was a medicine before it became a beverage. It is still the most popular medicine in China. Its healthy effects on the arteries, its ability to strengthen the immune system and its antibacterial, anti-cancer properties are known to Western sciences today. Similarly, the healing power of tears is an international leitmotif in literature and the media. Ho Chi Minh used to make a point of shedding a few tears when he appeared in public to speak to the people; it was largely those moving, wet speeches that endeared him so thoroughly to his audiences. Like Mao, he wrote poetry and was fully aware of the transformative power of songs, proverbs and folktales. In mythos, tears are at once a binder and a breaker. When cried by a true heart tears can break open a stone, they hold malefic forces at bay, they mend wounds, join souls and restore sight. In past and ongoing tales around the world, the shedding of tears continues to cause heartfelt reunions.

Tea is actually the very beverage that links the upper classes to the peasantry. Present in the most humble home and promoting well-being in simplicity and sobriety, it has been hailed by lovers and philosophers of tea as that which represents the true spirit of Asian democracy (Kazuko Okakura). In Japan where the art and ritual of tea was an intrinsic part of Zen ethics and aesthetics, people easily speak of a man "with no tea" or a man "with too much tea" inside in commenting on the lack or the excess of emotional subtleties in a person's character. Of great relevance, for example, is the importance given to a cup of tea in Buddhist lore. A Zen master's invitation to his student or to his visitor to "have a cup of tea" reaches deep and far in its immediate simplicity. As Zen master and activist Thich Nhat Hanh puts it, "You and the taste of tea are one . . . The tea is you, you are the tea . . . When one starts to distinguish [drinker and tea], the experience *disappears*."[2] Thus, the heart that hears the lone tear, hears the silent cry of the crowd.

Tears and other waters—rain, river, blood—as well as the art of waiting are inseparable in folklore and in love stories. They also play a creative, feature role in the national poem *The Tale of Kieu* and in Hoai's novel *The Crystal Messenger*; for without patience, tears and determination, none of these stories could find a peaceful ending. When asked about the current state of literature in Vietnam, one of the common answers encountered among writers is precisely: "We've gained permission to be sad! At least we can now weep without being gagged." Waiting is an indispensable state in relationships. It is said the one who knows how to wait, knows how to keep the spirit simple and pure. As the tale tells us, the fisherman's heart turned into a gem—an unusually translucent stone that immediately caught the eye of the mandarin himself. Some of the most beautiful and well-loved tales in Vietnam (*Truyen Trau Cau*, The Betel and the Areca Tree; *Hon Vong Phu* or The Mountain of Waiting, for example) deal directly with the question of debt in terms of waiting. In these, the person waiting and weeping in grief until death is usually turned into a stone or a mountain. As mentioned earlier in relation to the fisherman's unattainable love, *waiting while remaining loyal to the call of one's heart is what it takes to "win over" an impossible situation*. Such waiting is not passive; it has an active, dynamic quality to which Vietnam's history can easily attest. In the numerous examples it provides, waiting plays an important role in war strategies—the Battle of Dien Bien Phu with the French colonials is a famous example.

Children of Dragons and Immortals

Two lines in the *Kieu* poem allude to the tale of *The Love Crystal*: "*No tinh chua tra cho ai/ khoi tinh mang xuong tuyen-dai chua tan*" (Till I've paid off my debt of love to him/ my heart will stay a crystal in the Country of the Golden Sources). In relation to these lines, a literary critic (Van Hac) also relates an old event reported in the Annals of Love: a young woman fell in love with a merchant who left one day and never returned. The woman fell sick waiting and died. When her remains were exhumed, relatives found in her womb something hard and unbreakable. Raising it against the light, they could see a human image inside. Later, the merchant came back to see it for himself. He was moved to tears and as his tears dropped on the hard object, it dissolved into blood. The difference between the event recorded and the tale told is fascinating. Not only is one struck by the change effected on the gender of the person who waits and dies in grief (the image of a woman longing and waiting until death for her man's return is much more common) and on the profession of the man (which is a far cry from our man on water or the man of tea), one is also baffled by the general sinister feeling left by the event, which for me, hardly compares to the uplifting character of the tale.

What makes all the difference is the one element missing in the event: the song. Through the fisherman's voice, it is the power of art that awakens a young heart to the joys and sorrows of loving and longing. Music—especially when performed freely, knowing not whose ear it will strike—is the gift that brings to life the dormant forces in the listener. Reciprocally, listening attentively without preconceived knowledge of the singer endows the song with a powerful existence. By wanting to see, the maiden betrays love and her impatient gaze dooms the man to lose his very power to heal and enchant. The Look cancels out the Voice. Only in his song does Orpheus retain Eurydice. His forbidden but irresistible gaze causes Eurydice to sink back to darkness and to be lost twice over. In Kafka's version, by essentially shutting off his ears to resist the call of the Sirens, Ulysses is bound to the confinement of sight, and sight only. He never knew what their songs sounded like nor could he truly tell, as Kafka pointed out, whether the Sirens did sing or not after all. It was, in the end, the Silence of the Sirens that Kafka heard through Homer's words. Similarities can also be drawn here between the tale and the *Kieu* poem or Hoai's novel, for what constitutes their enduring power is not so much the story as the creative use, in the poem's case, of a rhythm unique to Vietnamese folk songs, and in the novel's case, of a local street slang whose rich and unusual tone speaks its profound disregard for bigoted conventions.

With the song comes the desire to exceed its limits, for if the maiden did not break the pact of sight and sound with the fisherman, the best part of the story (and the story itself) would be lost. Reality would be confined merely to the material world of what is immediately visible and audible. The debt of love would have to be carried indefinitely on to the Country of the Golden Sources—that is, beyond our lifetime, into the world of immortals and of the departed—what the West calls Hell. It is not by chance that popular memory prefers the princessly aura of a maiden and the cachet of a fisherman to that of a merchant. The pairing goes far back in time and in Vietnamese people's imagination. One can at first simply relate the choice of the fisherman to the fact that fishing, together with cultivating rice, is one of the main activities in Vietnam for the common man to earn his living. One can also place that choice in an international context of tale telling where the fisherman is an archetypal figure for a questing of the self that merges with the instinctual, unpredictable forces of nature. The love boat floats indefinitely on water; as soon as it careens into shore, the spell is gone and separation occurs.

For the Vietnamese, the pairing of the fisherman with the fairy-like maiden easily calls to mind the legend of our origins, according to which the Vietnamese people as known today are descendants of three generations of supernatural marriages. The first generation is traced back to Emperor De-Minh of China (grandson of Emperor Than-Nong—meaning "chief of agriculture"), who married an Immortal he met at the foot of Mountain Ngu Linh; the second generation to his son Kinh Duong Vuong, who wedded the daughter of a Dragon King; and the third to Vuong's son, our mythic father Lac Long Quan, King of Dragons, whose wife was Au Co, Daughter of Mountains and descendant of an Immortal. Our mythic mother Au Co gave birth through a pouch containing a hundred eggs, which, after hatching, became one hundred boys. Mythic Father agreed then with mythic Mother that since he was the son of dragons and she belonged to the family of fairies, they should divide the country into two, each ruling one half in mutual reliance—he leading fifty of their sons toward the sea, and she leading the fifty others toward the mountains. This was how Vietnam as a nation was said to have been founded, the home to both people from the flatlands and people from the highlands. (Although "immortal" and "fairy" are used interchangeably, immortal actually bears no supernatural connotation for, in Taoist terminology for example, the term refers to the enlightened sage whose spiritual training is carried out in the uninhabitable environment of mountains.) The vestiges from older times of our matriarchal society are also accounted for in the legend, as Fairy Mother was said to have established the rule of our earliest historical King Hung and given the historical name Van Lang to our country.

The legend is a unique attempt by our ancestors to inquire into the unknown sources of our four-million-year history and to create fables about a land whose mountains and rivers seem at times to relish unleashing their destructive forces upon the people. I was born third in a family of seven children. We are six girls and one boy, my brother being, very fortunately for him, the first and eldest child. We girls were the happy result of my mother's sustained but unsuccessful effort to repeat her first glorious birth; she used to be a zealous promoter of the infamous Vietnamese proverb that says "a hundred girls are not worth a single (teeny) penis." When expressing pride for their peers, Vietnamese happily make use of the popular expression *Con Rong Chau Tien* (children of Dragons, nephews of Fairies). One of the Vietnamese words for "country" or "nation" is *nuoc*, a word that, significantly enough, also means "water." It is also worth noting that for people who consider themselves to be descendants of Dragons and Immortals, the term they use to designate "people" or "countrymen" is *dong-bao*, meaning "issued from the same pouch." When addressing his audience, again, Ho Chi Minh never failed to invoke the power of this term: he usually started his speeches with a heartfelt, soul-stirring *Dong bao than men* (beloved blood brothers) rather than with the more distant and formal "Kinh thua quy-vi dong bao" (dear respected gentlemen and compatriots) of other Vietnamese presidents.

A small debt of love turns out to be a mountainous debt. At first, we may think it is the maiden who owes the fisherman, for he dies loving her without getting anything in return; later she succeeds in discharging the debt when she weeps over his crystallized love and is forgiven as the love cup dissolves. Then we may also think that the debt is mutual for, as the Voice of tradition might assert, all love encounters are predestined and when lovers come together, they are simply fulfilling a debt they have incurred in a previous life. As we go further, however, we may realize that the notion of debt, as with all notions, can be practiced in a shallow, passive way ("There's nothing to do, for everything is meant to be that way"); or it can feed a dynamic awareness and practice that will profoundly change our lives. African writers see into this when they assess that the cavernous actions of colonialism did not simply affect the living; they desecrated the world below, violating the dead in their rest, and their noxious impact continues unavoidably to resonate with present and future generations. Expanding, through our small stories, our understanding of time is to realize the past is also the beginning of a future. This, for example, is what ecologists and activists have contributed when they contest the short-term solutions adopted by official leaderships around the world without much thought for the magnitude of their small actions in time—geological time, physiological time, time in which the millennium is but a blink.

The Century of Forgiveness?

In the world of media, if AIDS is often linked up with Africa, drugs with South America, and terrorism with Islam, debt seems to be the fate of the Third World. National development policies are often directed to meet economic priorities without concern for the long-term effects on people and the environment. What is known as the debt crisis is in fact an old dance in the vicious circle of exploiter and exploited. Capital is borrowed by developing countries to finance ecologically destructive projects and to pay off their debts, these countries are cashing on natural resources for short-term export income. In other words, the debt has no limit. And in this era of globalization where failure and success bear the same name, borrowing money and getting into debt for life so as to have a home, a car or a computer of one's own is certainly a normalized practice in the private as well as the public sector of American life. Those of us who are slow to make use of the power of "plastic" (credit cards) are told that we are highly in need of counseling. In fact, the two biggest economies in the world are also the two most impressive debtors. Japan and America are deeply caught in the debt trap and are faring on fragile ground. The survival issue is not a Third World issue; it is a global issue and an issue of globalization. With the call for a reduction in worldwide economic activity—that is, in energy use and in overconsumption—it is hardly surprising that Vietnamese officials have been nervous about rapid development projects and that frustrations continue to determine much of the foreign investors' experience in Vietnam.

Tensions easily arise between those who expect Vietnam to abide by their standards of market "opening" and those who obsessively check and brake for fear of losing what they bitterly fought for. If the last two decades have seen Vietnam's economy expand, they have also witnessed uneven, stifling limits on media, artistic and economic activities—and with these, the pervasive problem of state corruption, which the guilty authorities, like those in China, attempt to solve by selecting a few sensational scapegoats. These were made to pay mercilessly for the unacknowledged, humongous debt that the government owed its people since the end of the war. The Tiananmen Square event in Beijing in 1989 and the turn of events in eastern and central Europe had haunted the old leadership. No wonder that an article in *The Economist* (July 29, 2000), complained about how the Vietnamese authorities had been treating its foreign investors the way most of us would react to our dentists: we know we have to open wide, but at the tiniest hint of discomfort, we react instinctually by clenching hard.

On the world map, demands for apologies and restitution for historical injustices have also grown widely over the past decades, to the irritation of many who feel that the current generation should not be made to accept and pay for a past they feel they are not responsible for. It is striking at first to recognize, through these reactions, how convincingly the same shallow logic continues to circulate and how strongly resistance can be built around such an issue as that of apology. For it is impossible, through the demands voiced, not to welcome the shift of consciousness in the struggle against social injustice. "Say Sorry," the sign simply reads. Fragile, absurd and seemingly derisive. Apparently the goal is not merely to obtain compensation, to appeal for a single group, or to serve any single pre-determined finality, but more importantly, to reclaim what may be called "post-human agency" in history by asking that the debt be acknowledged in its symbolic scope for the well-being of past, present and future generations. This accounted, for example, for the striking support that 250,000 concerned citizens showed in Sydney for Australia's Aboriginal people by massively participating in the May 28th 2000 walk of atonement. *The deeper and wider you go, the older the story.*

As human history substantiates, it sometimes takes a catastrophe, whether "natural" or man-made, to pull us together across endless security walls and boundaries. (And yet . . .) Our massive drive for destruction could then find itself mirrored by an equally immense capacity for forgiveness and hope. Reeducation camps, rehabilitation camps, concentration camps, annihilation and extermination camps: all the death camps in which forgiveness is said to have died once and for all. However, it is in the face-to-face with the impossible—the irreparable and the non-negotiable—that the possibility of forgiveness arises, and just when one feels one has reached the end of the road in making the last step, one finds oneself walking on, making the impossible step, turning aside, turning about, turning toward. One truly forgives only when one squarely faces the unforgivable. The grand gesture of public reconciliation and redemption has its strategic purpose, but it has little to do with forgiveness. For the debt of love knows no limit; what it requires exceeds all judicial logic and processes. After Japan had finally offered its apologies to Korea, a Japanese artist eagerly told me: "The twenty-first century may very well be the century of forgiveness."

Other Than Myself,
My Other Self

First published in *Traveller's Tales*, eds. G. Robertson, M. Mash,
L. Tickner, J. Bird, B. Curtis & T. Putnam (London: Routledge,
1994), pp. 9–26.

Every voyage can be said to involve a re-siting of boundaries. The traveling self is here both the self that moves physically from one place to another, following "public routes and beaten tracks" within a mapped movement; and, the self that embarks on an undetermined journeying practice, having constantly to negotiate between home and abroad, native culture and adopted culture, or more creatively speaking, between a here, a there, *and* an elsewhere.

Traveling Tales

A public place around a train station. In Marrakech. In Fez. In a city of words, told by a husky voice. In a body full of sentences, proverbs, and noises. There, a story is born. This body is a fountain. Water is an image. The source travels. A crowd of children and women wait in line in front of the well. Water is scarce. Stories heap up at the bottom of the well . . .

These images land in disorder. They reach me from afar and speak to me in my mother tongue, an Arabic dialect riddled with symbols. This language, which one speaks but does not write, is the warm fabric of my memory. It shelters and nourishes me.

Can it withstand the travel, the shifts, the extreme mobility in the new clothes of an old foreign language? Out of modesty, it retains its secrets and only rarely does it give itself in. It is not it that travels. It is I who carry a few fragments of it.[1]

The source moves about; it travels. Tahar Ben Jelloun's fountain-body unfolds through movements of words, images of water, sensations of mother-memory, and sounds of traveling fractions. These come in disorder, he wrote, doubting that Mother's language at home—or Language—will ever be able to withstand the mobility of the journey. Never quite giving itself in, however, Language remains this inexhaustible reservoir from which noises, proverbs and stories continue to flow when water is scarce. Thus, it is not "It" that travels. It is "I" who carries here and there a few fragments of It. In this cascade of words, where and which is the source finally? I or It? For memory and language are places both of sameness and otherness, dwelling and traveling. Here, Language is the site of return, the warm fabric of a memory, and the insisting call from afar, back home. But here also, there, and everywhere, language is a site of change, an ever-shifting ground. It is constituted, to borrow a wise man's words, as an "infinitely interfertile family of species spreading or mysteriously declining over time, shamelessly and endlessly hybridizing, changing its own rules as it goes."[2]

It is often said that writers of color, including anglophone and francophone Third World writers of the diaspora, are condemned to write only autobiographical works. Living in a double exile—far from the native land and far from their mother tongue—they are thought to write by memory and to depend to a large extent on hearsay. Directing their look toward a long bygone reality, they supposedly excel in reanimating the ashes of childhood and of the country of origin. The autobiography can thus be said to be an abode in which the writers mentioned necessarily take refuge. But to preserve this abode, they would have to open it up and pass it on. For, not every detail of their individual lives bears recounting in such an "autobiography," and what they choose to recount no longer belongs to them as individuals. Writing from a representative space that is always politically marked (as "colored" or as "Third World") they do not so much remember for themselves as they remember in order to tell. When they open the doors of the abode and step out of it, they have, in a sense, freed themselves again from "home." They become a passage, start the travel anew, and pull themselves at once closer and further away from it by telling stories.

A shameless hybrid: I or It? Speaker or Language? Is it Language, which produces me, or I who produce language? In other words, when is the source "here" and when is it "there"? Rather than merely enclosing the above writers in a place recollected from the past, the autobiographical abode propels them forward to places of the present—foreign territories, or the lands of their adopted words and images. "The writer writes so that he no longer has a face," T. B. Jelloun remarked. "One relapses into memory as one relapses into childhood, with defeat and damage. Even if it were only to prevent such a fall, the writer sees to it that he is in a layer of 'future memory,' where he lifts and displaces the stones of time."[3] Journeying across generations and cultures, tale telling excels in its powers of adaptation and germination; while with exile and migration, traveling expanded in time and space becomes dizzyingly complex in its repercussive effects. Both are subject to the hazards of displacement, interaction and translation. Both, however, have the potential to widen the horizon of one's imagination and to shift the frontiers of reality and fantasy, or of Here and There. Both contribute to questioning the limits set on what is known as "common" and "ordinary" in daily existence, offering thereby the possibility of an elsewhere-within-here, or -there.

An African proverb says, "A thing is always itself and more than itself." Tale telling brings the impossible within reach. With it, I am who It is, whom I am seen to be, yet I can only feel myself there where I am not, vis-à-vis an elsewhere I do not dwell in. The tale, which belongs to all countries, is a site where the extraordinary takes shape from the reality of daily life. Of all literary genres, it is the one to circulate the most, and its extreme mobility has been valued both for its local specificity and for its capacity to speak across cultural and ethnic boundaries. To depart from one's own language of origin, to be able to acknowledge that "the source moves about," to fare like a foreigner in this language, and to return to it via its traveling fragments is also to learn how to be silent and to speak again, differently. T. B. Jelloun opens, for example, his well-known tale of Moha the Fool, Moha the Sage (*Moha le fou, Moha le sage*) with an epigraph which reminds the reader of the political death of a man and goes on to affirm: "It doesn't matter what the official declarations say. A man has been tortured. To resist the pain, to overcome the suffering, he resorted to a strategy: to recollect the most beautiful remembrances of his short life."[4] And on this statement unfolds the telling of the man, as captured and transmitted by Moha, or as written by Jelloun himself.

A Stranger in a Strange Country

"He's a stranger," Louise said joyfully. "I always thought so—he'll never really fit in here."

"How long are you going to keep me prisoner?" he asked.

"Prisoner?" answered the director, frowning. "Why do you say prisoner? The Home isn't a jail. You weren't allowed to go out for several days for reasons of hygiene, but now you're free to go wherever you like in the city."

"Excuse me," said Akim, "I meant to say: when can I leave the Home?"

"Later," said the director, annoyed, "later. And besides, Alexander Akim, that depends on you. When you no longer feel like a stranger, then there will be no problem in becoming a stranger again."[5]

Much has been written on the achievements of exile as an artistic vocation, but as a traveling voice from Palestine puts it, exile on the twentieth-century scale and in the present age of mass immigration, refugeeism, and displacement "is neither aesthetically nor humanistic-ally comprehensible." This "irremediably secular and unbearably historical" phenomenon of untimely massive wandering remains "strangely compelling to think about but terrible to experience" (Edward Said).[6] For people who have been dispossessed and forced to leave for an uncertain destiny, rejected time and again, returned to the sea or to the no man's land of border zones; for these unwanted expatriated, it seems that all attempts at exalting the achievements of exile are but desperate efforts to quell the crippling sorrow of homelessness and estrangement. The process of rehabilitation which involves the search for a new home appears to be above all a process by which people stunned, traumatized and mutilated by the shifts of event that have expelled them from their homelands learn to adjust to their sudden state of isolation and uprootedness.

Refugeeism, for example, may be said to be produced by political and economic conditions that make continued residence intolerable. The irreversible sense of "losing ground" and losing contact is, however, often suppressed by the immediate urge to "settle in" or to assimilate in order to overcome the humiliation of bearing the too-many-too-needy status of the homeless-stateless alien. The problem that prevails then is to be accepted rather than to accept. "We are grateful. We do not want to be a nuisance," said a Vietnamese male refugee in Australia who, while feeling indebted to his host country, believes that only in Vietnam can a Vietnamese live happily.[7] Or else, "We are a disturbance. That's the word. Because we show you in a terrible way how fragile the world we live in is . . . You didn't know this in your skin, in your life, in every second of your life," said a less grateful Cambodian woman refugee in France who considers Paris to be, in the racial distances it maintains, "a city of loneliness and ghosts."[8] Intensely connected with the history and the politics that have erupted to displace them, refugees are unwanted persons whose story has been an embarrassment for everyone, as it "exposes power politics in its most primitive form . . . the ruthlessness of major powers, the brutality of nation-states, the avarice and prejudice of people."[9] Dispossessed not only of their material belongings but also of their social heritages, refugees lead a provisional life, drifting from camps to camps, disturbing local people's habits and destabilizing the latter's lifestyle when they move into a neighborhood. However they are relocated, they are a burden on the community. On the one hand, migrant settlements can turn out to be "centers of hopelessness" which soon become "centers of discontent." On the other hand, those who succeed in resettling are blamed for usurping the work from someone else, and those who fail to secure happiness in their adopted lands are accused of being ungrateful, worsening thereby a situation in which exclusionary policies have been advocated on the ground that the rich host nations will soon be put in "the poorhouse" by the flood of refugees—because "they multiply."[10]

Great generosity and extreme gratitude within sharp hostility; profound disturbance for both newcomers and old-timers: the experience of exile is never simply binary. If it's hard to be a stranger, it is even more so to stop being one. "Exile is neither psychological nor ontological," wrote Maurice Blanchot. "The exile cannot accommodate himself to his condition, nor to renouncing it, nor to turning exile into a mode of residence. The immigrant is tempted to naturalize himself, through marriage for example, but he continues to be a migrant."[11] The one named "stranger" will never really fit in, so it is said, joyfully. To be named and classified is to gain better acceptance, even when it is a question of fitting in a no-fit-in category. The feeling of imprisonment denotes here a mere subjection to strangeness as confinement. But the Home, as it is repeatedly reminded, is not a jail. It is a place where one is compelled to find stability and happiness. One is made to understand that if one has been temporarily kept within specific boundaries, it is mainly for one's own good. Foreignness is acceptable once I no longer draw the line between the others and myself. First assimilate, and then be different within permitted boundaries. "When you no longer feel like a stranger, then there will be no problem in becoming a stranger again." As you come to love your new home, it is thus implied, you will immediately be sent back to your old home (the authorized and pre-marked ethnic, gender or sexual identity) where you are bound to undergo again another form of estrangement. Or else, if such a statement is to be read in its enabling potential, then, unlearning strangeness as confinement becomes a way of assuming anew the predicament of deterritorialization: it is both I and It that travel; the home is here, there, wherever one is led to in one's movement.

Wanderers across Language

Our present age is one of exile. How can one avoid sinking into the mire of common sense, if not by becoming a stranger to one's own country, language, sex and identity? Writing is impossible without some kind of exile. Exile is already in itself a form of *dissidence* . . . a way of surviving in the face of the *dead father* . . . A woman is trapped within the frontiers of her body and even of her species, and consequently always feels *exiled* both by the general clichés that make up a common consensus and by the very powers of generalization intrinsic to language. This female in exile in relation to the General and to Meaning is such that a woman is always singular, to the point where she comes to represent the singularity of the singular—the fragmentation, the drive, the unnameable.[12]

Perhaps, "a person of the twentieth century can exist honestly only as a foreigner,"[13] suggests Julia Kristeva. Supposedly a haven for the persecuted and the homeless, Paris, which has offered itself to many stateless wanderers as a second home ever since the late nineteenth century, is itself a city whose houses, as Walter Benjamin described them, "do not seem made to be lived in, but are like stones set for people to walk between."[14] The city owes its liveliness to the movements of life that unfold in the streets. Here, by choice or by necessity pedestrians, passers-by, visitors, people in transit can all be said to "dwell" in passageways, strolling through them, spending their time and carrying on most of their activities outside the houses, in the intervals of the stonework. Such a view of Paris would contribute to offsetting the notion of home and dwelling as a place and a practice of fixation and sameness. For after all, where does dwelling stop? In a built environment where outside walls line the streets like inside walls, and where the homey enclosures are so walled off, so protected against the outside that they appear paradoxically set only "for people to walk between," outsiders have merely brought with them one form of outsideness: that very form others who call themselves insiders do not—out of habit—recognize as their own insideness.

"Modern Western culture," remarks Said, "is in large part the work of exiles, émigrés, refugees."[15] If it seems obvious that the history of migration is one of instability, fluctuation and discontinuity, it seems also clear for many Third World members of the diaspora that their sense of group solidarity, of ethnic and national identity has been nourished in the milieus of the immigrant, the refugee and the exiled. Here, identity is a product of articulation. It lies at the intersection of dwelling and traveling and is a claim of continuity within discontinuity (and vice-versa). A politics rather than an inherited marking, its articulation and re-articulation grows out of the very tension raised between these two constructs—one based on socio-cultural determinants and the other, on biological ones. The need to revive a language and a culture (or to reconstitute a nation out of exile as in the case of the Palestinian struggle) thus develops with the radical refusal to indulge in exile as a redemptive motif, and to feel uncritically "at home in one's own home," whether this home is over there or over here. Such a stance goes far beyond any simplistic positive assertions of ethnic or sexual identity, and it is in this difficult context of investigation of self that, rather than constituting a privilege,

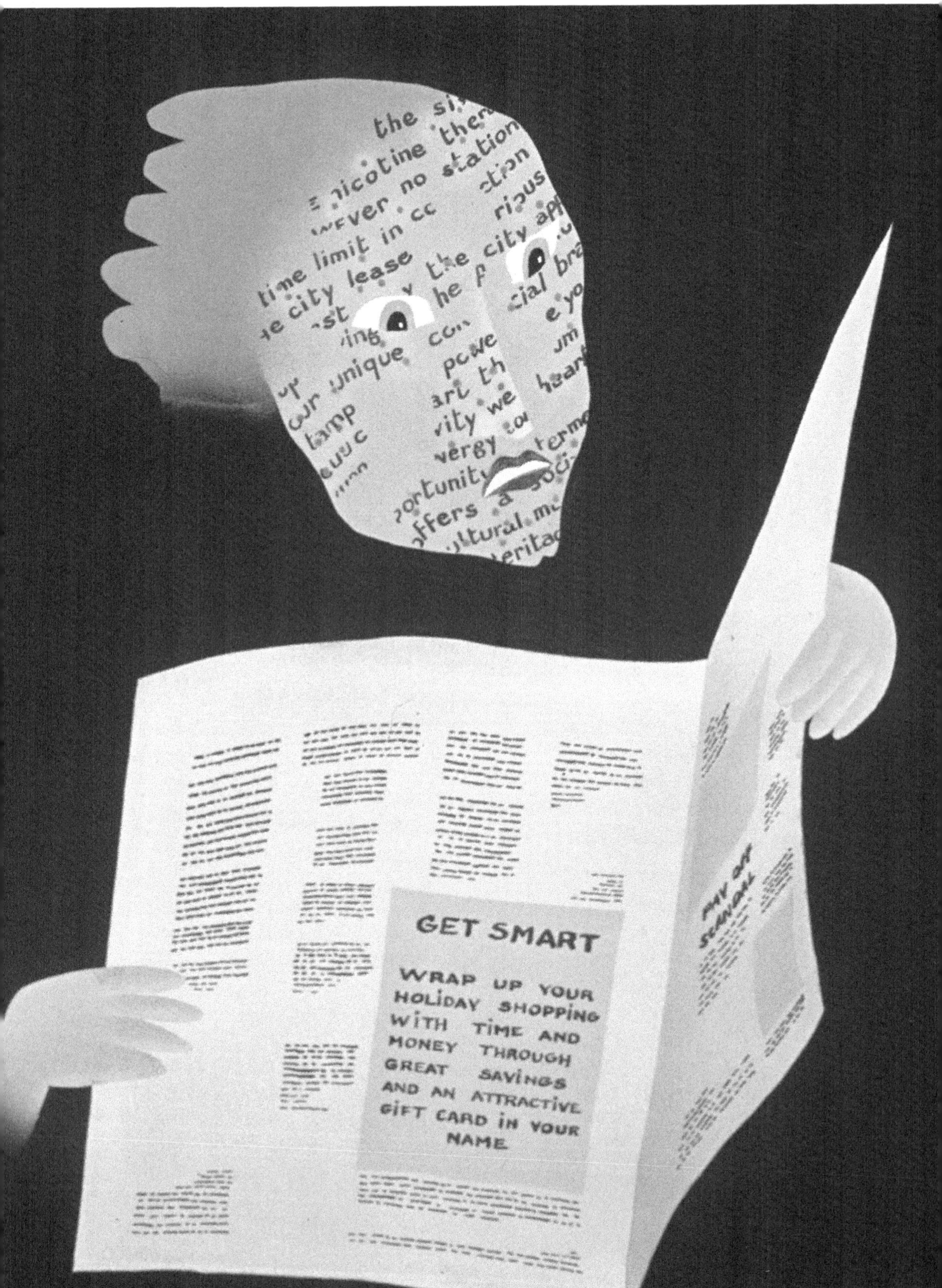
GET SMART
WRAP UP YOUR HOLIDAY SHOPPING WITH TIME AND MONEY THROUGH GREAT SAVINGS AND AN ATTRACTIVE GIFT CARD IN YOUR NAME

exile and other forms of migration can become "an *alternative* to the mass institutions that dominate modern life."[16]

Home and language tend to be taken for granted; like Mother or Woman, they are often naturalized and homogenized. The source becomes then an illusory secure and fixed place, invoked as a natural state of things untainted by any process or outside influence (by "theory" for example), or else, as an indisputable point of reference whose authority one can unfailingly rely on. Yet, language can only live on and renew itself by hybridizing shamelessly and changing its own rules as it migrates in time and space. Home for the exile and the migrant can hardly be more than a transitional or circumstantial place, since the "original" home neither can be recaptured nor can its presence/absence be entirely banished in the "remade" home. Thus, figuratively but also literally speaking, traveling back and forth between home and abroad becomes a mode of dwelling. Every movement between here and there bears with it a movement within a here and a movement within a there. In other words, the *return* is also a journey into the layer of "*future memory*" (Jelloun). The to-and-fro motion between the source and the activity of life is a motion within the source itself, which makes all activities of life possible. As regards Mother and Woman, she remains representatively singular (on His terms)—despite the very visible power of generalization implied in the capitals M and W used here. For, unless economical necessity forces her to leave the home on a daily basis, she is likely to be restrained in her mobility—a transcultural, class- and gender-specific practice that for centuries has not only made traveling quasi impossible for women, but has also compelled every "traveling" female creature to become a stranger to her own family, society and gender.

It is said that when Florence Edenshaw, a contemporary Haida elder, was asked, "What can I do for self-respect?" by a woman anthropologist who interviewed her and on whom Edenshaw's dignity made a strong impression, Edenshaw replied: "Dress up and stay home." Home seems to take on a peculiarly ambiguous resonance; so does the juxtaposition of "dress" and "stay." One interpretation suggests that such a statement reflects the quiet dignity of members of non-state societies who rarely travel for the sake of some private quest, and deliberately risk themselves only when it is a question of the whole community's interest. Home then is as large as one makes it.[17] The profound respect for others starts with respect for oneself, as every individual carries the society within her. Read, however, against the background of what has been said earlier on Mother and Woman, Edenshaw's answer can also partake in the naturalized image of women as guardians of tradition, keepers of home and bearers of Language. The statement speaks of/to their lack of mobility in a male economy of movement. Women are trapped (as quoted) within the frontiers of their bodies and their species, and the general cliché by which they feel exiled here is the common consensus (in patriarchal societies) that streets and public places belong to men. Women are not supposed to circulate freely in these male domains, especially after dark (the time propitious to desire, "the drive, the unnameable" and the unknown), for should anything happen to them that violates their physical well-being, they are immediately said to have "asked for it" as they have singularly "exposed" themselves by turning away from the Father's refuge. Yet, Edenshaw's statement remains multi-leveled. It ultimately opens the door to a notion of self and home that invites the outside in, implies expansion through retreat, and is no more a movement inward than a movement outward, toward others. The stationariness conveyed in "stay home" appears artificial—no more than a verbal limit—as "stay" also means "reach out."

For a number of writers in exile, the true home is to be found, not in houses, but in writing. Such a perception may at first reading appear to contradict Kristeva's affirmation that "writing is impossible without some kind of exile." But, home has proven to be both a place of confinement and an inexhaustible reservoir from which one can expand. And exile, despite its profound sadness, can be worked through as an experience of crossing boundaries and charting new ground in defiance of newly authorized or old canonical enclosures—"a way of surviving in the face of the *dead father*." Critical dissatisfaction has brought about a stretching of frontiers; home and exile in this context become as inseparable from each other as writing is from language. Writers who, in writing, open to research the space of language rather than reduce language to a mere instrument in the service of reason or feelings, are bound like the migrant to wander from country to country. They are said to be always lost to themselves, to belong to the foreign, and to be deprived of a true abode since, by their own passionate engagement with the tools that define their activities, they disturb the classical economy of language and representation, and can never be content with any stability of presence. Nothing remains unmoved; everything safe and sound is bound to sink somewhere in the process.

Their Country Is My Country

Love, miss and grieve. This I can't simply deny. But I am a stranger to myself and a stranger now in a strange land. There is no arcane territory to return to. For I am no more an "overseas" person in their land than in my own. Sometimes I see my country people as complete strangers. But their country is my country. In the adopted country, however, I can't go on being an exile or an immigrant either. It's not a tenable place to be. I feel at once more in it and out of it. Out of the named exiled, migrant, hyphenated, split self. The margin of the center. The Asian in America. The fragment of Woman. The Third within the Second. Here too, Their country is My country. The source continues to travel. The predicament of crossing boundaries cannot be merely rejected or accepted. Again, if it is problematic to be a stranger, it is even more so to stop being one. Colonized and marginalized people are socialized to always see more than their own points of view, and as Said phrases it, "the essential privilege of exile is to have, not just one set of eyes but half a dozen, each of them corresponding to the places you have been . . . There is always a kind of doubleness to that experience, and the more places you have been the more displacements you've gone through, as every exile does. As every situation is a new one, you start out each day anew."[18]

Despite the seemingly repetitive character of its theme and variations, the tale of hyphenated reality continues its hybridizing process. It mutates in the repercussive course of its reproduction as it multiplies and displaces itself from one context to another. It is, in other words, always transient. But transience is precisely what gives the tale its poignancy. Having grown despite heavy odds in places where it was not meant to survive, this poetry of marginalized people not only thrives on, but also persists

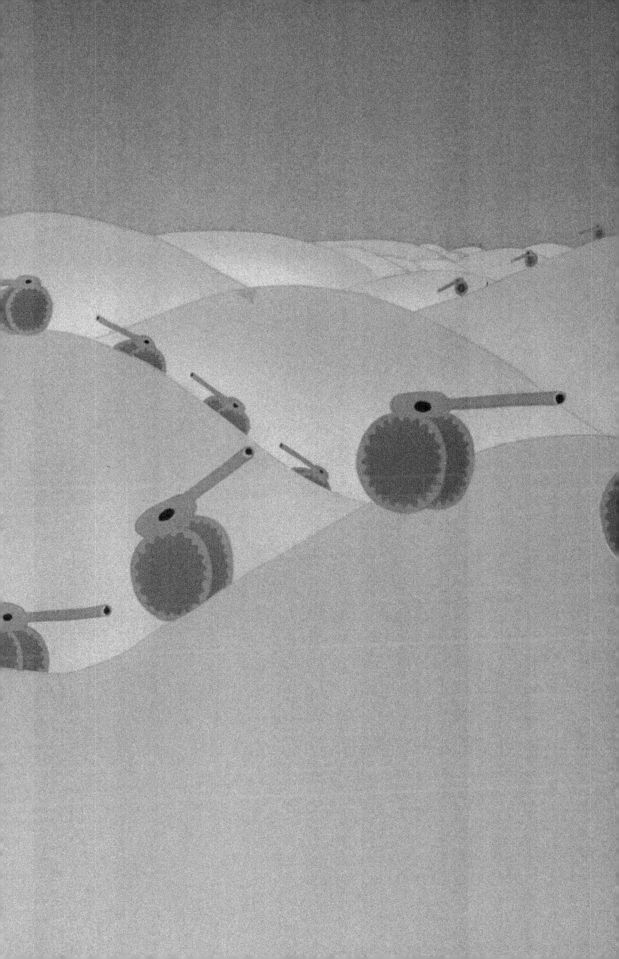

in holding its ground (no matter how fragile this ground proves to be) and sometimes even succeeds in blooming wildly, remarkable in its strange beauty and fabulous irregularity. Some familiar stories of "mixed blessings" in America continue to be the following:

So, here we are now, translated and invented skins, separated and severed like dandelions from the sacred and caught alive in words in the cities. We are aliens in our own traditions; the white man has settled with his estranged words right in the middle of our sacred past.

(Gerald Vizenor)

I could tell you how hard it is to hide right in the midst of White people. It is an Art learned early because Life depends on dissimulation and harmlessness. To turn into a stone in the midst of snakes one pays a price.

(Jack Forbes)

Our people are internal exiles. To affirm that as a valid experience, when all other things are working against it, is a political act. That's the time when we stop being Mexican Americans and start being Chicanos.

(Judy Baca)

There is no doubt in my mind that the Asian American is on the doorstep of extinction. There's so much out-marriage now that all that is going to survive are the stereotypes. White culture has not acknowledged Asian American art. Either you're foreign in this country, or you're an honorary white.

(Frank Chin)

Sometimes/ I want to forget it all/ this curse called identity/ I want to be far out/ paint dreams in strange colors/ write crazy poetry/ only the chosen can understand/ But it's not so simple/ I still drink tea/ with both hands.

(Nancy Hom)

If you're in coalition and you're comfortable, then it is not a broad enough coalition.

(Bernice Johnson Reagon)

The possibilities of meaning in "I" are endless, vast, and varied because self-definition is a variable with at least five billion different forms . . . [T]he I is one of the most particular, most unitary symbols, and yet it is one of the most general, most universal as well.

(Cornelia Candelaria)

I've avoided calling myself "Indian" most of my life, even when I have felt that identification most strongly, even when people have called me an "Indian." Unlike my grandfather, I have never seen that name as an insult, but there is another term I like to use. I heard it first in Lakota and it refers to a person of mixed blood, a metis. In English it becomes "Translator's Son." It is not an insult, like half-breed. It means that you are able to understand the language of both sides, to help them understand each other.

(Joseph Bruchac)[19]

Translators' sons and daughters, or more redundantly, the translators' translators. The source keeps on shifting. It is It that travels. It is also I who carry a few fragments of it. Translations mark the continuation of the original culture's life. As it has been repeatedly proven, the hallmark of bad translation is to be found in the inability to go beyond the mere imparting of information or the transmittal of subject matter. To strive for likeness to the original—which is ultimately an impossible task—is to forget that for something to live on, it has to be transformed. The original is bound to undergo a change in its afterlife. Reflecting on the translator's task, Benjamin remarked that: "just as the tenor and significance of the great works of literature undergo a complete transformation over the centuries, the mother tongue of the translator is transformed as well. While a poet's words endure in his own language, even the greatest translation is destined to become part of the growth of its own language and eventually to be absorbed by its renewal." Defined as a mode serving to express the *relationship* between languages (rather than an equation between two dead languages), translation is "charged with the special mission of watching over the maturing process of the original language and the birth pangs of its own."[20]

The Blue Frog

Identity is largely constituted through the process of othering. What can a return to the original be, indeed, when the original is always already somewhere other than where it is thought to be; when "stay home" also means "reach out," and native cultures themselves are constantly subject to intrinsic forms of translation? Here, Third is not merely derivative of First and Second. It is a space of its own. Such a space allows for the emergence of new subjectivities that resist letting themselves be settled in the movement across First and Second. Third is thus formed by the process of hybridization which, rather than simply adding a here to a there, gives rise to an elsewhere-within-here/-there that appears both too recognizable and impossible to contain. Vietnamese francophone poet and novelist Pham Van Ky, for example, raises the problematics of translated hyphenated realities specifically in the following terms:

Mother. A word released, a word with precise contours, which crushes me but does not cover me up entirely, but does not articulate my Parisian existence; already a decision hardens within me . . . this abyss of secrets, reticences, obscurities, hollow dreams and foul haze between Mother and me: nothing clear, a series of disagreements, of bitter trails where grass never grows, a chain of vague pains jumping at my wrist and around my chest, seeking to restrain my breathing and the circulation of my blood . . . In the Bois de Vincennes, I reread the cablegram: Mother seemed near me. I tried to draw her closer to me: she became distant again. Because I had forgotten about her, did I feel less tied to her by life? Why conceal her from myself? She had carried me in her hemorrhage; I did not pull out a single hair, which was not a bit, hers.[21]

Another instance of working with between-world reality is that of Elaine K. Chang who, in an attempt to situate herself (via an essay significantly entitled: "A Not-So-New Spelling of My Name: Notes Toward (and Against) a Politics of Equivocation"), has this unique story of traveling metaphor to offer:

Within the North American "Asian community," I am sometimes called a banana; it is said that I may have a yellow skin, but I am white on the inside. I am considered ashamed of my yellowness, insofar as I apparently aspire to master the language, culture and ideology of white people. *Banyukja* is . . . a Korean translation of the Spanish *Vendida*—the Korean who has forgotten, or never known, her heritage, her language . . . I cannot properly answer to these names, especially to and in a language I have lost. I cannot tell those for whom I am a banana, or worse a *banyukja*, that my exile from them is not entirely self-imposed, that I am not ashamed and have not forgotten. Nor can I respond in so many English or broken Korean words that the ignorance they ascribe to men, the silence they expect from me, themselves cooperate to estrange me: that what I do understand of what they say serves to alienate me . . . If I could rename myself, . . . I think I would have to select a figure not female, not divine, not even human: the blue frog. My mother's story about the blue frog was my favorite childhood story. The blue frog never does anything his mother tells him to do; in fact he does precisely the opposite. I pestered my mother to tell the story over and over; each time she told it, the frog-mother's requests and the blue frog's responses seemed to become more outrageous. The ending, however, remained soberly the same. Loving and knowing her son, and knowing she is about to die, the frog-mother makes her last request: that her son bury her body in the river—of course thinking her son, due to his contrary nature, will bury her in the ground. When his mother dies, however, the blue frog is so remorseful for his life-long disobedience that he chooses to observe her final wishes. So every time it rains, the blue frog cries, thinking that his mother's body is washing away in the river.

It wasn't until I was considerably older, and she had not told the story for years, that I asked my mother if she remembered the little blue frog. Confused at first, she remembered after I'd recapitulated the basic plot structure. Blushing, my mother informed me that the frog was not, in fact, blue; she had not yet mastered colors in English when she first told me the story. Old as I was, I was crushed by this information: it was all along just some ordinary green frog. What had compelled me about this particular frog—this frog whose story quite accurately . . . resembles the story of my relationship with my mother—was his blueness . . . I would invoke the blue frog as my inspiration because of this coding and recoding of the color of his skin; the ambiguity of his color registers the sorts of small but significant ironies that distinguish my experience as a westernized child of immigrant parents. My mother shared with me a Korean folktale that acquired something new in its translation into English . . . The blue frog is a (by-) product of cultural and linguistic cross-fertilization—a small and mundane one, to be sure, but one that I would take as my emblem . . . Do blue frogs have a place in academic discourse?[22]

Tale telling is what it takes to expose motherhood in all its ambivalence. The boundaries of identity and difference are continually repositioned in relation to varying points of reference. The meanings of here and there, home and abroad, third and first, margin and center keep on being displaced according to how one positions oneself. Where is "home"? Mother continues to exert her power from afar. Even in her absence she is present within the teller, his blood, his source of life. From one generation to another, mothers are both condemned and called upon to perfect their role as the killjoy keepers of home and of tradition. In Kristeva's fable of dissidence, Mother (with capital M) may be said to partake in the "mire of common sense" (common to whom?) and to represent Meaning as established by the "dead father." Therefore, it is by resisting Her powers of generalization that a woman becomes a stranger to her own language, sex and identity. In Jelloun's tale of time, Mother is the benevolent traveling source that, in fact, does not travel on her own. She is, rather, the transmitter of "a body full of sentences, proverbs and noises," and the originator of the "warm fabric of [his] memory" that "shelters and nourishes [him]." Like language, mother (with small m) retains her secrets and it is through her son that she travels and continues to live on—albeit in fragments.

For Pham Van Ky, Mother is what he fiercely rejects without feeling any less tied to her by life. In a conventional gender division, she—the guardian of tradition—represents his Oriental, Vietnamese, Confucian past and the Far East over there; while he—the promoter of modernity—can go on representing change and progress, and the Far West over here. But as he admits to himself, mother can neither be discarded nor easily appropriated: "I did not pull out a single hair which was not a bit hers." In fact, the traveling seed has never had an original location that could simply be returned to. For Elaine Chang, Mother is the imperfect transmitter of a folktale whose voyage in time, across language and generation has allowed it to acquire something new in its translation. The coding and recoding of the skin color of the frog speak to the sadness (/blueness) of both the daughter's and the frog's inappropriate experience of translation. In both cases, mistranslation results from a two-way imperfection in the triangular relationship of mother, child and language. The source is never single and the home-and-abroad or land-and-water trajectory is a mutual voyage into self and other. Traveling in what appear to be opposite directions, the two parties only meet when "meet" also comes to mean "lose"—that is, when mother or the story can no longer be returned to as redemptive site. Understanding and consciousness emerge in one case, when the frog realizes its mistake in carrying out a literal translation of his mother's request after she has passed away; and in the other case, when the daughter's natural identification with the blue frog comes to an end to make way for a "politics of equivocation" in the articulation of hyphenated identity. The ability to assume anew the responsibility of translation thereby opens up to an elsewhere, at once not-yet- and too-well-named within the process of cultural and linguistic cross-fertilization.

I, the Mis-seer

Every voyage is the unfolding of a poetic. The departure, the crossover, the fall, the wandering, the discovery, the return, the transformation. If traveling perpetuates a discontinuous state of being, it also satisfies, despite the existential difficulties it often entails, one's insatiable need for detours and displacements in postmodern culture. The complex experience of self and other (the all-other within me and without me) is bound to forms that belong but are neither subject to "home," nor to "abroad;" and it is through them and through the cultural configurations they gather that the universe over there and over here can be named, accounted for, and become narrative. Travelers' tales do not only bring the over-there home, and the over-here abroad. They do not only bring the far away within reach, but also contribute, as discussed, to challenging the home and abroad/dwelling and traveling dichotomy within specific actualities. At best, they speak to the problem of the impossibility of packaging a culture, or of defining an authentic cultural identity.

For cultures whose expansion and dominance were intimately dependent upon the colonial enterprise, traveling, as part of a system of foreign investment by metropolitan powers, has largely been a form of culture collecting aimed at world hegemony. In their critical relation to such a journeying practice, a number of European writers[23] have thus come to see in traveling a socio-historical process of dispossession that leads the contemporary traveler to a real identity crisis. Through this "nightmare of degradation," the Traveler seems to have become so banal, outdated and disintegrated in certain images he projects that it is not unusual to ask whether he is still . . . a possibility. One among some fifty million globetrotters, the Traveler maintains his difference mostly by despising others like him. I sneeze at organized tours, for the things I see in the Wild or in the remote parts of the world, are those You can't see when You abide by pre-paid, ready-made routes. Furthermore, You don't see all that I know how to see, even if You go to the same places. In the arguments used here to preserve one's difference, there is an eager attempt to define one's activities by negating them. The role of the traveler as privileged seer and knowledgeable observer has thus become quasi impossible, for it is said that the real period of Traveling always seems to be already past, and the other travelers are always bound to be "tourists."[24]

The search for "micro-deserts," the need to ignore or the desire to go beyond the beaten tracks of pre-packaged tours is always reactivated. Traveling here inscribes itself as a deviance within a circularly saturated space. Adventure can only survive in the small empty spaces of intervals and interstices. As soon as something is told, there is nothing more to discover and to tell, so it is believed. All that remains for the real Traveler is "the privilege of a certain look, in the margin of the Standard Point of View as signaled in the tourist Guides." Constantly evoked, therefore, are the blindness and myopia of the Tourist whose voracity in consuming cultures as commodities has made hardship and adventure in traveling a necessary part of pre-planned excitement rather than a mere hindrance. Cultural tourism is thus said to challenge the dichotomy that separates the expert Ethnologist from the non-expert Tourist. "The traditional Traveler's tragedy is that he is an imitable and imitated explorer." Therefore, in order not to be confused with the Tourist, the Traveler has to become clandestine. He has to *imitate* the Other, to hide and disguise himself in an attempt to inscribe himself in a counter-exoticism that will allow him to be a non-Tourist—that is, someone who no longer resembles his falsified other, hence a stranger to his own kind.[25]

Ironically enough, it is by turning himself into another falsified other (in imitating the Other) that the Traveler succeeds in marking himself off from his falsified other (the Tourist). He who is easily imitable and imitated now takes on the role of the imitator to survive. The process of othering in the (de) construction of identity continues its complex course. Rather than contributing to a radical questioning of the privileged seer, however, the Traveler's "identity crisis" often leads to a mere change of appearance— a temporary disguise whose narrative remains, at best, a Confession. As discussed earlier, striving for likeness to the original without being powerfully affected by the foreigner (the Other) is the hallmark of bad translation. The Traveler as imitator may perform the task of a faithful reproducer of meaning, but to become a (good) translator, he would have "to expand and deepen his language by means of the foreign language."[26] To travel can consist in operating a profoundly unsettling inversion of one's identity: I become me via an other. Depending on who is looking, the exotic is the other, or it is I. For the one who is off- and outside culture, is not the one over there whose familiar culture I am still a part of, or whose unfamiliar culture I come to learn from. I am the one making a detour with myself, having left upon my departure from over here not only a place but also one of my selves. The itinerary displaces the foundation; the background of my identity, and what it incessantly unfolds is the very encounter of self with the other—other than myself and, my other self.

In traveling, one is a being-for-other, but also a being-with-other. The seer is seen while s/he sees. To see and to be seen constitute the double approach of identity: the presence to oneself is at once impossible and immediate. "I can't produce by myself the stranger's strangeness: it is born from [at least] two looks."[27] Traveling allows one to see things differently from what they are, differently from how one has seen them, and differently from what one is. These three supplementary identities gained via alterity are in fact still (undeveloped or unrealized) gestures of the "self"—the energy system that defines (albeit in a shifting and contingent mode) what and who each seer is. The voyage out of the (known) self and back into the (unknown) self sometimes takes the wanderer far away to a motley place where everything safe and sound seems to waiver while the essence of language is placed in doubt and profoundly destabilized. Traveling can thus turn out to be a process whereby the self loses its fixed boundaries—a disturbing yet potentially empowering practice of difference.

> "The word is more important than syntax . . . It is the blanks that impose themselves . . . I am telling you how it happens, it is the blanks that appear, perhaps under the stroke of a violent rejection of syntax . . . [T]he place where it writes itself, where one writes . . . is a place where breathing is rarefied, there is a diminution of sensorial acuity . . ."
>
> "Would a man, in his sexuality, show the blank just like that? Because it's also sexual, this blank, this emptiness."
>
> "No, I don't think so; he would intervene. I myself do not intervene."[28]

It seems clear, for writers like Marguerite Duras who lets herself return to "a wild country" when she writes, that one can only gain insight by letting oneself go blind as one gropes one's way through the oversaid and the all-too-clear of one's language. "Men are regressing everywhere, in all areas," she remarked. "The theoretical sphere is losing influence . . . it should lose itself in a reawakening of the senses, blind itself, and be still." For scarcely has an important event been experienced before men, always eager to act as theoretical policemen, "begin to speak out, to formulate theoretical epilogues, and to break the silence . . . [H]ere silence is precisely the sum of the voices of everyone, the equivalent of the sum of our collective breathing . . . And this collective silence was necessary because it would have been through this silence that a new mode of being would have been fostered." Duras called such arresting of the flow of silence "a crime and a masculine one," for if it has in innumerable cases stifled the voices of the marginalized others, it has in her own case certainly made her "nauseous at the thought of any activism after 1968."[29]

If the space of language is to resonate anew, if I am to speak differently, He must learn to be silent—He, the Traveler who is in me and in woman. For s/he who thinks s/he sees best because s/he *knows* how to see is also this conscientious "mis-seer to whom the tree hides the forest."[30] Without perspectives, deaf and myopic to everything that is not microscopic, the non-tourist-real-traveler operates, often unknowingly, in a realm of diminished sensorial acuity. On the one hand, s/he develops a highly refined ear and eye for close readings, but remains oblivious to the landscape and the "built environment" which make the traveler-seer's activities possible and communicable. On the other hand, deliberate mis-seeing is necessitated to bring about a different form of seeing. When the look is "a three-way imperfection" developed between the subject observed, the subject observing, and the tools for observation, the encounter is likely to resonate in strangely familiar and unpredictable ways. The translator transforms while being transformed. Imperfection thus leads to new realms of exploration, and traveling as a practice of bold omission and minute depiction allows one to (become) shamelessly hybridize (d) as one shuttles back and forth between critical blindness and critical insight. I-the Seer is bound to mis-see so as to unlearn the privilege of seeing, and while I travel, what I see in every ordinary green frog is, undeniably, my blueness in the blue frog. In the zest of telling, I thus find myself translating myself by quoting all others. The traveling tales.

II

boundary event

Between Refuse and Refuge

An Acoustic Journey

First published in *Rethinking Borders*, ed. J. Welchman (U.K.
& U.S. versions) (London: Macmillan Press Ltd.; Minneapolis:
University of Minnesota Press, 1996), pp. 1–17.

> Every people felt threatened by a people without a country
> —Jean Genet, *Prisoner of Love*

In the current political and cultural landscape, a crucial shift in the (dis/re) articulation
of identity and difference has been emerging—and maturing. Such articulations remain
informed by an awareness of both the enabling and disenabling potentials of the divisions
within and between cultures. Constantly guarded, reinforced, destroyed, set up, and reclaimed,
boundaries not only express the desire to free/to subject one practice, one culture, one
national community from/to another, but also expose the extent to which cultures are
products of the continuing struggle between official and unofficial narratives—those
largely circulated in favor of the State and its policies of inclusion, incorporation and
validation, as well as of exclusion, appropriation and dispossession. Yet, never has one
been made to realize as poignantly as in these times how thoroughly hybrid historical
and cultural experiences are, or how radically they evolve within apparently conflictual
and incompatible domains, cutting across territorial and disciplinary borders, defying
policy-oriented rationales and resisting the simplifying action of nationalist closures.
The named "other" is never to be found merely over there and outside of oneself, for
it is always over here, between Us, within Our discourse that the "other" becomes a
nameable reality. Thus, despite all the conscious attempts to purify and exclude, cultures
are far from being unitary, as they have always owed their existence more to differences,
hybridities and alien elements than they really care to acknowledge.

Midway to Nowhere

As the twentieth century has been referred to as "the century of refugees and prisoners,"
the 1980s might well be termed the decade of refugees and the homeless masses. No
longer an extraordinary occurrence that requires a temporary solution, refugeeism has

become a regular feature of our times. Today it is visible almost everywhere, including Africa, the Middle East, Latin America, Asia and Europe. Multifaceted "border wars" continue to be waged on an international scale accompanied by an unavoidable hardening of frontiers, tightening of control, and multiplication of obstacles and aggressions at the borders themselves. A matter of life or death for many, the act of crossing overland and oversea to seek asylum in unknown territories is often carried out—especially in mass flight—as an escape alone, with no specific haven of refuge in mind. Thus, the creation of refugees remains bound to the historical forces and political events that precipitate it. It reflects a profound crisis of the major powers, the repercussions of which are made evident in the more specific, devastating crisis of the millions of individuals directly affected. The myopic view that the refugee problem is Their problem and one on which Our taxpayer's money should not be wasted is no longer tenable. The tragedy of tidal waves of people driven from their homes by forces beyond their control keeps on repeating itself as victims of power re-alignments, cross-border hostilities and orgies of so-called "ethnic cleansing" continue to grow to alarming proportions, and detention camps proliferate on the world map without drawing more than fitful, sporadic attention from the international community.

How does a journey start? What un/certainties compel one to take up again the by-now-familiar question of "Those Who Leave" and to depart anew through the conditions of 'the Border'—a 'place' so widely and readily referred to in the last few years that it already runs the risk of being reduced to yet another harmless catchword expropriated and popularized among progressive thinkers? To ask the question, here, is already to answer it. To speak about the concept of border crossing as a major theme in contemporary cultural politics is, in a way, further to empty it, get rid of it, or else let it drift—preventing it thereby from both settling down and being "resettled." One is bound through speaking and writing to assert one's ability to displace all attempts—including one's own—to rehabilitate key concepts, for the politics of the word or the "verbal struggle" as Mao called it, will never end. Words have always been used as weapons to assert order and to win political combats; yet, when their assertions are scrutinized, they reveal themselves, above all, as awkward posturing, as they often tend to blot out the very reality they purport to convey. The listener or reader is then invited to engage in the vertiginous art of reading not so much between the lines as *between the words* themselves.

> *Whole nations don't become nomads by choice or because they can't keep still. We see them through the windows of aeroplanes or as we leaf through glossy magazines. The shiny pictures lend the camps an air of peace that diffuses itself through the whole cabin, whereas really they are just the discarded refuse of 'settled' nations. These, not knowing how to get rid of their 'liquid waste', discharge it into a valley or on to a hillside, preferably somewhere between the tropics and the equator . . .*
>
> *We oughtn't to have let their ornamental appearance persuade us the tents were happy places. We shouldn't be taken in by sunny photographs. A gust of wind blew the canvas, the zinc and the corrugated iron all away, and I saw the misery plain.*[1]

The journey starts with the discomfiting memory of the "discarded refuse of settled nations" which Jean Genet evoked in his attempt to recapture the years he spent with

Palestinian soldiers in Jordan and Lebanon. *Refuge, refugee, refuse* . . . Genet's writing of his travel across identities and his erotic encounter with the "other"—or more specifically the Palestinians (previously it was the Algerians and the Black Panthers)—appeared in a volume titled *Un Captif amoureux.* Significantly enough, the 'accurate' English translation of this title would have to be found somewhere between 'prisoner of love' and 'prisoner in love,' embracing the passive–active action of both capturing and loving. This movement back and forth between maintaining/creating borders and undoing/passing over borders characterizes Genet's relationship with writing as well as with the people to whom he was passionately committed from the late 1960s until his death in 1986. His suicidal skepticism (isn't every critical autobiographical writing a way of surviving suicidally?), deployed with subtle humor, does not only translate itself in the refusal to romanticize a struggle, its setting and its people, but also in the way the writer positions himself within a "we" who, as in the quoted passage, safely "see them through the windows of aeroplanes" and on the pictures of "glossy magazines."

Entry into or exit from refugee status is, in many ways, neither voluntary nor simply involuntary. *I saw the misery plain.* In the past, attempts to reclassify this "liquid waste" have always been appropriately carried out according to the interests of the settled nations involved. The historical and official adaptation of such terms as "displaced person," "illegal immigrant" or "voluntary immigrant—rather than "refugee"—proved, for example, as in the case of the Boat People, to be a useful device through which the host society could either endorse arguments by those at home who opposed giving entry to the influx of unwanted aliens; or deny the problem of refugees by hastily declaring them "resettled" and hence equivalent to voluntary migrants. It seems, therefore, adequate to say that the resistance of many refugees to their being reclassified in a "voluntary" category was not a resistance merely to termination of direct assistance (as was often asserted among researchers and social workers), but rather to the denial of the state of indeterminateness and of indefinite unsettlement that characterizes the refugee's mode of survival. Here, refugeeism differs from voluntary immigration in that it does not have a *future* orientation—the utopia of material, social or religious *betterment*. Official re-labeling in this instance means primarily deciding who is worthy of humanitarian assistance from the international community, and who is not. Again, what constantly seems to be at stake is the problem of identification and of "alignment" in the wider (religious, ideological, cultural, as well as class-, race-, and gender-determined) senses of the term. *Refuse*. Which side? But above all, which boundaries? Where does one place one's loyalties? How does one identify oneself?

> *As you walk or drive through the refugee camps, one phenomenon noticed after awhile is the constant movement within the camps . . . The strolling seemed endless and the constant patternless flux of this tide of humanity was lulling, nearly hypnotic to watch.*[2]

Of the many movements of flight and migration witnessed across international borders, it was noted (not without patronizing) that: "The story of the Indochina refugees is the story of people *refused*—refused first and most painfully by their own governments, refused too often by neighboring countries where they sought temporary asylum and refused, initially at least, by the West and Japan, the only nations with the capacity and the heart to save them."[3] Although feelings of gratitude in the process of successful readjustment are never missing among Those Who Leave, the "midway to nowhere" malaise of the transit and camp period has not in any way ended with resettlement. (The expression "midway to nowhere" was used to characterize the transit situation of the Vietnamese refugees before they became immigrants to a specific country.[4]) To the accusation that refugees are a burden to taxpayers, the dutiful response obtained among the "unwelcome guests" has been, faithfully enough, that: "Most refugees have only one hope: 'to have a job and become a tax payer.'"[5] Without endorsing the ostracizing connotations of a psychiatric diagnosis such as the "displacement syndrome" associated with psychological disorders among refugees, one can further state that this specific but elusive form of surviving is not a transitional malaise limited to "long stayers"—refugees whose prolonged stay in the camp (five to six years or more) has often led to a situation of deteriorating morale.

The long-stayers' agonizing bind between *waiting* in uncertainty for the unknown and longing with fear for *returning* home continues to be experienced, albeit in different forms, by those happily "resettled." A well-known example is that of the Hmong people among whom the "sudden death syndrome" was said to prevail: a person, regardless of age or state of health, dies a sudden death during his or her sleep at night, without any apparent reason. Since the phenomenon could not be explained in medical terms despite the autopsies that were carried out, the phenomenon has remained unsalvageable to Western science, and was unfailingly spoken about in the press as one of those mysterious, inscrutable phenomena of the Orient. Considered to be a reaction to the stress of both displacement and integration, this death-during-sleep is understood among the Vietnamese as the outcome of acute sadness: *buon thoi ruot*, or sad to the extent that one's bowels rot, as a common Vietnamese expression goes. A slightly different interpretation of the same phenomenon exists, however, among the Hmong who say that the soul has taken flight during dreamtime and has here embarked on: a no-return journey.

"You Are the Battleground"

> They knew just how to keep us in our place.
> And the logic was breathtakingly simple: If you win, you lose.
> —Henry Louis Gates, Jr., *Loose Canons*

From one category, one label to another, the only way to survive is to refuse. Refuse to become an Integra table element. Refuse to allow names arrived at transitionally to become stabilized. In other words, refuse to take for granted the naming process. To this end, the intervals between *refuge* and *refuse*, *refused* and *refuse*, or even more importantly between *refuse* and *refuse* itself, are constantly played out. If, despite their relation, noun and verb inhabit the two very different and well-located worlds of designated and designator, the space in-between them remains a surreptitious site of movement and passage whose open, communal character makes exclusive belonging and long-term residence undesirable, if not impossible. Passage: the state of metamorphosis; the conversion of

water into steam; the alteration of an entire musical framework. Intervals-as-passage-spaces pass further into one another, interacting radically among themselves and communicating on a plane different from the one where the 'actions' of a scenario are explicitly situated. In intensity and *resonance* (more than in distance actually covered), the journey here continues.

. . . *caught in the crossfire between camps*
while carrying all five races on your back
not knowing which side to turn to, run from

. . . *In the Borderlands*
    you are the battleground
    where enemies are kin to each other;
    you are at home, a stranger,
    the border disputes have been settled
    the volley of shots have shattered the truce
    you are wounded, lost in action
    dead, fighting back;

. . . *To survive the Borderlands*
    you must live sin fronteras
    be a crossroads.

(Gloria Anzaldúa,
Borderlands/La Frontera)[6]

"Never does one feel as solitary as when fleeing in the midst of millions," a refugee once said. A solitude born in/with the multitude is a solitude that remains potentially populous—utterly singular and yet collective, always crowded with other solitudes. By refusing to partake in categories of both the Refused and the Integrated, even while refusing and integrating, it may seem that one gives oneself no place on which to stand, nowhere to head for. But to resort here—whether positively or negatively—to the popularized 'infinite shifting of the signifier' (often equated with the endless sliding/slurring of liberal-pluralist discourse) is merely to borrow a ready-made, an all-too-dwelled-on expression that is bound to lose its relevance when irrelevantly used. Raising the doubt, however, invites contribution to the current struggle around positionalities (identities and differences); a struggle which, by its unsettling controversies, has at times been referred to as "the war of position" in cultural politics. *You are the battleground/ where enemies are kin to each other.*

Much has been written in the last few years on the totalizing nature of the logics of borders and of warring essences. Yet the questioning of oppositional stances that aim exclusively at reversing existing power relations is constantly at work among marginalized groups themselves. What has been "a necessary fiction" to allow for the emergence of counter-narratives by second-class citizens seems to be no more and no less than a strategy in the complex fight for and against "authorized marginality." As Stuart Hall puts it, "Once you enter the politics of the end of the essential black subject you are plunged headlong into the maelstrom of a continuously contingent, unguaranteed, political argument and debate: a critical politics, a politics of criticism."[7] For many members of long-silenced cultures, if the claim to the rights of (self-) representation has been in some ways empowering, the shift to the politics of representation proves to be still more liberating, for what is renounced is simply an exclusive form of fictionalizing: namely, the habit of asserting/assigning identity by staking out one's/the other's territory, Africanizing the African or Orientalizing the Oriental, for example, and reproducing thereby the confine-and-conquer pattern of dominance dear to the classic imperial quest.

Permanent unsettlement within and between cultures is here coupled with the instability of the word, whose old and new meanings continue to graft onto each other, engaged in a mutually transformative process that displaces rather than simply denies the traces of previous grafting. *You are at home, a stranger.* In the historical context of ethnic discrimination and devalorization, re-appropriation of a negative labeling as an oppositional stance in cultural politics often functions as a means both to remind and to get rid of the label's derogative connotations. At best, such a stance makes use of existing boundaries only to counter-politicize them, leading thereby to a concurrent tightening and loosening of pre-established limits. *You are wounded, lost in action/ dead, fighting back.* The question as to when one should 'mark' oneself (in terms of ethnicity, age, class, gender, or sexuality for example) and when one should adamantly refuse such markings continues to be a challenge. For answers to this query remain bound to the specific location, context, circumstance, and history of the subject at a given moment. Here, positionings are radically transitional and mobile. They constitute the necessary but arbitrary closures that make political actions and cultural practices possible.

The difficulties faced in the struggle around positionalities can be found in the current conflicted debate over political representation between members of marginalized and centralized cultures. As has been pointed out, political criticism usually works by demonstrating what a text *could* mean (the possibilities in the production of meaning) while insinuating what a text *does* mean (the issue of its reception and political effectivity).[8] Thus, discussions of the "politics of *interpretation*" often turn out to be complex, indirect interpretations of the "politics of *interpreters*." Uneasiness in "trading on this ambiguity" has been repeatedly voiced by members on both sides; but, with the critical work effected in cultural politics, it has become more and more difficult to approach a subject by asking 'what' or even 'how' without also asking 'who,' 'when,' and 'where'? Power has always arrogated the right to mark its others while going about unmarked itself. Within an economy of movement, the dominant self, the 'universal subject,' represents himself as flexible, explorative, 'uncolored' and unbounded in his moves, while those caught in the margin of non-movement are represented as 'colored,' authentic—that is, uncomplicatedly locatable and custom-bound. Always eager to demarcate the others' limits, We only set up frontiers *for ourselves* when Our interest is at stake.

While for many members of dominant groups, designating one's white ethnicity (to mention only one positioning) still appears largely 'useless' and 'redundant,' for members of the marginalized groups, signaling one's non-white ethnicity remains as questionable or even as objectionable as denying it. *If you win, you lose.* When multiculturalism and cultural diversity (as defined by the West's liberal tradition) become sanctioned, the danger faced, expectedly enough, is that of control and containment. Authorized marginality means that the production of 'difference' can be supervised, hence recuperated, neutralized and depoliticized. Unless they 'force' their entry, therefore, marginalized 'interpreters' are allowed into the Establishment only so long as the difference they offer proves to be locatable and evaluable within the ruling norms. As Henri Louis Gates disarmingly puts it: "Once scorned, now exalted . . . It takes all the fun out of being oppositional when someone hands you a script and says, 'Be oppositional, please—you look so cute when you're angry.'"[9]

Reflecting back on the Black Panthers of the late sixties, Jean Genet offered another view of the movement that further contributes to the discussion here of the politics of representation. Like the Palestinian people, the African American people, as Genet saw it, are without land and have no territory of their own. Since "land is the necessary basis for nationhood," it provides a place from which war can be fought and to which warriors can retreat. Being able neither to take refuge from, nor to stage a revolt in, the ghetto, nor, again, to march out from the ghetto to battle on white territory—all American territory being under White Americans' control—the war the Panthers waged would have to "take place elsewhere and by other means: in people's consciences." Thus, the Black Panthers' first line of attack was launched by sight, and by effecting visible change in the way they saw themselves (hence in the way other people saw them). Metamorphosing the Black community while undergoing a metamorphosis in themselves, they emerged from nonvisibility into extravisibility. Not only did they build an unforgettable image of their own people ("Black is Beautiful"), they also brought to consciousness the link between every people that had been oppressed and robbed of its history and its legends ("All Power to the People"). Their strategy of war was to reaffirm and to push to ever-greater *excess* their African identity, and their weapons may be said to consist of: leather jackets, revolutionary hair-dos, and *words*—delivered in a "gentle but menacing tone." Despite the fact that they were heading for death or prison, the change they brought about with their metamorphosis had made the Black struggle "not only visible, but crystal clear." The dramatic image deliberately created "was a theater both for enacting a tragedy and for stamping it out—a bitter tragedy about themselves, a bitter tragedy for the Whites. They aimed to project their image in the press and on the screen until the Whites were haunted by it. And they succeeded." In the end, "the Panthers can be said to have overcome through poetry."[10]

They won by losing, and they lost by winning. The forceful rejection of marginality thrives here on a vital attraction to marginality. The conflict is only in name. "The black words on the white American page are sometimes crossed out or erased. The best disappear, but it's they that make the poem, or rather the poem of the poem."[11] Words and images can be starting points for actions; together they form memory and history. The powerful image wrested from the reality of despair continues to live on beyond the individuals who created it. With no program to head for, however, the movement quickly wore out, as the spectacle of Blackness always ran the risk of being consumed as (colorful) *spectacle*. According to Martin Luther King, the slogans, which enchanted both black and white youths, were necessary rallying cries for Black identity.[12] But above all, they were painful, reactive attempts to romanticize a cry of disappointment through the advocacy of an impossible separatism. For Genet, "Power to the People" soon came to be a thoughtless habit and, despite its seductive power, the Panthers' flashy image was too quickly accepted and "too easily deciphered to last."[13] But if, in his moments of reflexive speculation, Genet saw the Panthers as "flamboyant youngsters" who "were frauds," and their spectacle as "mere figment," he also openly recognized that his "whole life was made up of unimportant trifles cleverly blown up into acts of daring."[14] (Genet's own tumultuous life and gay identity have been made a spectacle both in his work and in the works of other well-known writers such as Sartre and Cocteau.) The awareness of his being "a natural sham," invited to go first with the Panthers, and then with Palestinian soldiers to spend time "in Palestine, in other words *in a fiction*," compelled him to go on playing the role of "a dreamer inside a dream," or more acutely, of "a European saying to a dream, 'You are a dream—don't wake the sleeper!' "[15]

Nations and fictions. A man who spent his life drifting as an outcast from shore to shore, who explicitly refused to identify himself with his country of birth, and whose metamorphosis had turned him into a stranger at home (France and the West having become "utterly exotic" to his eyes), decided to engage all his energies to supporting the political dreams/realities of marginalized and dispossessed peoples. This is hardly surprising. *The soul has taken flight during dreamtime and has embarked on a no-return journey.* Yet he who persistently rejected any homeland, found himself paradoxically attracted to those (here the Palestinian people) who long for a territory of their own and whose ongoing struggle centers on an unswerving claim to the homeland from which they were driven. A claim? Perhaps the word again serves to blot out another reality, for longing here is also specifically refusing to be 'resettled.' In fact, 'home' in itself has no fixed territory; depending on the context in which it appears, it can convey the concept of settlement or unsettlement. The refusal to move from "tents to huts" is a refusal to let oneself be duped into moving not only from one form of dispossession to another, but also from a mode of transitional dwelling or of resistance, to a mode of fixed dwelling or of compliance. Better service, better control.

The paradox, if any, is only in name. What made Genet draw the line—a line that matters here and now—and take up a position by the side of the dispossessed was, not so much the voice of justice in its logic of naming, as the emotions it conveyed—or better, its musical accuracy: "*I had greeted the revolt as a musical ear recognizes a right note.*"[16] Thus, despite his affectionate support of the Black Panther movement and passionate commitment to the Palestinian resistance, Genet can be said to have written *lovingly*: he wrote not merely to praise, but, more so, to expose. To expose both the reality under "the canvas, the zinc and the corrugated iron," and the acute consciousness of himself as not quite belonging ("a pink and white presence among them"), "attracted but not blinded," crossing but only to *return*, standing perpetually *at the border*, trying not to pass for one of them nor to speak on their behalf. *Justice at its best is love correcting everything that stands against love (Martin Luther King).*[17] So goes the story of this dreamer whose fourteen years of commitment to the revolution were haunted by the memory of a little house in Irbid where he had spent one single night with a Palestinian soldier and his mother: "An old man traveling from country to country, as much ejected by the one he was in as attracted by the others he was going to, rejecting the repose that comes from even modest property, was amazed by the collapse that took place in him . . . [A]fter a very long time, when he thought he'd really divested himself of all possessions, he was suddenly invaded, one can only wonder via what orifice, by a desire for a house, a solid fixed place, an enclosed orchard. Almost in one night he found himself carrying inside him a place of his own."[18]

A Matter of Tuning

> Meter is dogmatic, but rhythm is critical
>
> —Gilles Deleuze and Felix Guattari, *A Thousand Plateaus*

like indians
dykes have fewer and fewer
someplace elses to go
so it gets important
to know
about ideas and
to remember or uncover
the past
and how the people
traveled
all the while remembering
the idea they had
about who they were
indians, like dykes
do it all the time
. . . we never go away
even if we're always
leaving
because the only home
is each other
they've occupied all
the rest
colonized it; an
idea about ourselves is all
we own
     (Paula Gunn Allen,
Some Like Indians Endure)[19]

Living at the borders means that one constantly treads the fine line between positioning and de-positioning. The fragile nature of the intervals in which one thrives requires that, as a mediator-creator, one always travels transculturally while engaging in the local "habitus" (collective practices that link habit with inhabitance) of one's immediate concern. A further challenge faced is that of assuming: assuming the presence of a no-presence, and vice-versa. One's alertness to the complexities of a specific situation is always solicited as one can only effect a move by acknowledging, without occupying the center, one's location(s) in the process of engendering meaning. Even when made visible and audible, such locations do not necessarily function as a means to install a (formerly denied or unexpressed) subjectivity. To the contrary, its inscription in the process tends above all to disturb one's sense of identity. How to negotiate, for example, the line that allows one to commit oneself entirely to a cause and yet not quite belong to it? To fare both as a foreigner on foreign land and as a stranger at home? *Be a crossroads.* Amazed by the collapse that is perpetually taking place in oneself (to adapt Genet's words), one sees oneself in constant metamorphosis, as if driven by the motion of change to places so profoundly hybrid as to exceed one's own imagination. Here, the space of representation is necessarily what also becomes a "content" in the emergence of "form."

For Gloria Anzaldúa, life in the Borderlands has been equated with *intimate terrorism*: "Woman does not feel safe when her own culture, and white culture are critical of her."[20] She has to confront both those who have alienated her and those for whom she remains the perennial "alien." Terrorized by the wounds they/she inflict/s on her/self, she is likely to assume at least two exiles: the external and the internal one, if she is to live life on her own. "I am a turtle, wherever I go I carry 'home' on my back . . . [T]hough 'home' permeates every sinew and cartilage in my body, I too am afraid of going home. Though I'll defend my race and culture . . . I abhor some of my culture's ways, how it cripples its women, *como burras*, our strengths used against us, lowly *burras* bearing humility with dignity."[21] *They've occupied all/ the rest.* Unable simply to return home to her mother culture where she has been injured as *woman*, nor to settle down on the other side of the border (in the lost homeland, *El Otro Mexico*) as *alien* in the dominant culture, she thus sets about to divest (their) terrorism of its violently anti-feminist, anti-lesbian, anti-colored legacy. *The only home/ is each other.* She "surrenders all notion of safety, of the familiar . . . [and] becomes a *nahual*, able to transform herself into a tree, a coyote, into another person." Taking the plunge, she puts to motion a new *mestiza* culture based on an emerging "racial, ideological, cultural and biological cross-pollinization, an 'alien' consciousness, *una concienca de mujer* . . . a consciousness of the Borderlands."[22]

> *as a Black feminist I ask myself and anyone who would call me sister, Where is the love?*
> (June Jordan)[23]

Love, hatred, attraction, repulsion, suspension: all are music. The wider one's outlook on life, it is said, the greater one's musical hearing ability. The more displacements one has gone through, the more music one can listen to. Appeal is a question of vibration. Was it Novalis who mentioned, "Every illness is a musical problem"? Isn't it by the help of vibrations, often via the power of the word and the touch, that illnesses can be cured? For, in many parts of the world, music is not an art. It is a language—and for an attuned ear, the first language. One finds music in listening. In moments of isolation, alone with oneself or with nature. In moments of collective tuning, in the midst of a crowd or while working with a communal issue. *We never go away/ even if we're always/ leaving.* "Meeting across difference always requires mutual stretching," wrote Audre Lorde, "and until you *can* hear me as a Black Lesbian feminist, our strengths will not be truly available to each other as Black women . . . I am a Black Lesbian, and I *am* your sister."[24] A dive of the self into the self and out, unmeasured and unchartered, often leads to the realization that one does not in/un-habit one unitary, or two contradictory worlds. Some of us live only in a world external to ourselves, so that when we speak, we only speak *out*; when we point, we point to the world out there, from a largely unquestioned place of subjectivity. Others among us think we live in two contrasting (East–West) worlds and when we speak, we speak within binary systems of thought. The 'other' is thus always located outside Us. When incorporated, it can only be recognized if it stands in opposition to the known and the familiar. But the dive up and down within self-set boundaries leads nowhere, unless self-set devices to cross them are also at work. Moving from flight to flight, more of us have come to see, not only that we live in many worlds at the same time, but also that these worlds are, in fact, all in the same place—the place each one of us is here and now.

In Asian cultures, it is commonly said that one should not receive a word by hearing it only with one's ears when one can develop the ability to receive the same word also with one's mind and heart. Caught in a shifting framework of articulation, words and concepts undergo a transformative process where they continue to resonate upon each other on many planes at once, exceeding thereby the limit of that very plane where all the 'actions' are supposed to be carried out. To develop the ability to receive with more than one's eyes or ears is to expand that part of oneself which is receptive but can remain atrophied, almost closed, when its potential lies dormant. For even though every one is endowed with such a potential, almost no one is 'naturally' tuned to this pitch of acute intensity where music, flowing both outside and within us, defines all activities of life. Wrote a thinker of the West, "the faculty of being 'receptive,' 'passive,' is a precondition of freedom: it is the ability to see things in their own right, to experience the joy enclosed in them, the erotic energy of nature . . . This receptivity is itself the soil of creation: it is opposed, not to productivity, but to *destructive* productivity."[25] *Meeting and parting at crossroads, we each walk our own path.*

Receptivity is a two-way movement. To be receptive, one has to turn oneself into a responsive mold. The simultaneously passive–active process enables one to be tuned by one's changing environment while also developing the ability to tune oneself independently of any environment. Music here is both what makes creation possible and the means of receiving it. *How the people/ traveled/ all the while remembering/ the idea they had/ about who they were.* In the Chinese Yin and Yang principle, such a movement of receptivity is nothing other than the fundamental movement of inhalation and exhalation that sets into motion and sustains all of life. Also called the Two Ch'i or the Breaths of Heaven and Earth, the Yin and Yang concept is one in which, significantly enough, the two motions inward and outward or upward and downward is actually the same and one motion. Thus, Two does not necessarily imply separateness for it is never really equated with duality, and One does not necessarily exclude multiplicity for it never expresses itself in one single form, or in uniformity. The perpetual motion of life and death is represented with acuity in the emblem of the disk of the *T'ai Chi.* Here, the Yin and Yang are visually reproduced in the light and dark halves of the circle and, notably, these are not divided by a straight line, but by a curve, whose S-shape ingeniously depicts the constant ebb and flow, or rhythmic alternation, the forward/renewed and backward/decline movement, that regulates the fabric of life down to its smallest details. It stands for the active and passive, masculine and feminine, positive and negative forces found, for example, in mountain and water, sun and moon, South and North, motion and rest, advance and return. And the naming can go on, multiplied a thousandfold.

Refuse. Return. Resonance sets into motion and sustains all creative processes. It makes all the difference. As John Cage used to say, poetry is not prose simply because it is formalized differently, or because of its content and ambiguity, but rather, because it allows "musical elements (time, sound) to be introduced into the world of words."[26] The inhaling and exhaling is the work of rhythm, or of Breath, manifested as voice, sound, word—whether audible or silent, spoken or written, outside or within. And rhythm is what lies in-between night and day and makes possible their process of alternation in alterity. Thanks to the rhythm of the heart, mind, body and soul can be poetically tuned. The effect of music is to solicit a situation of perpetual inter-tuning, in which the rhythm of another person is constantly adopted and transformed while the person untunes him/herself to vibrate into the music that is being performed. What attracts a listener to music is, above all, rhythm and resonance in the making. How it comes and goes, leaving its marks, changing the course of things, and resonating intensely on the listener at times when it is least expected. Rhythm is then always vital, for it always departs from meter and measure to link those critical moments of passage when things unfold while in metamorphosis, and when the process of tuning oneself consists of finding not only the transitional pitch necessitated at a given moment—motion—but also one's own (many-and/in-one-) pitch—rest. The struggle of positionalities may in the end be said to depend upon the accurate tuning of one's many selves. *Where is the love?*

A finale. Although he dressed, behaved and lived like a Buddhist priest, Japanese poet Matsuo Basho likened himself to something at best named "bat," being as he put it, "neither priest nor layman, bird nor rat, but something in between."[27]

Nature's r

A Musical Swoon

First published in *Futurenatural*, ed. George Robertson et al. (London: Routledge, 1996), pp. 86–104.

As long as there is a future, all truth will be partial.
—Cheikh Amidou Kane

all time is a now-time . . . The past is the future.
—Patricia Grace

We sense the fatal taste of material paradise. It drives one to despair, but what should one do? *No future.*
—Jean Baudrillard

The mind lags behind nature.
—Gilles Deleuze and Felix Guattari

Nature. Make it a small, not a capital N, and nature applies to almost everything that is nameable. Take off both capital N and small n, and what remains is an *ature-* fragment whose music and meaning change radically with the substitution of a single opening consonant. M, for example: Mature. Or as in French: *mature, rature, sature.* Now delete the r, and the sound, incomplete, would have to remain suspended, *na-tu* . . . unable to carry through its musical term. For a sign to unsettle itself and to break loose from its fixed representations, duration is made audible, space between syllables is spelled out, and time, deferred. Delete, replace, return, then let be. The r in nature is the gray zone between sound and sense. To leave both the n and the r in, therefore, is not to revert to nature in its 'original,' non-dismembered state, but rather, to listen again carefully, critically, ec-static-ally, to its musical intervals.

Perceptible to the ear and yet hardly articulated, the r in nature is always half-muted, half-pronounced. It is the very phoneme whose pronunciation remains in parentheses [nache(r)]—that is, somewhere between a sound and a silence. In listening to a song, a poem, a phrase, or even a single word, one listens to both their marked and non-marked beats. What retains one's attention is the way meaning and sound come together and move apart from one another, ceaselessly closing the gaps while producing new gaps between themselves, finding thereby their beginnings and endings in creative rhythm. More than the use of pauses and interruptions, the boundary event that makes one hold one's breath is here the dying fall—the fragile moment when in the shift to a lower note, sound becomes sigh and word fades to breath. The musical swoon (in nature's r) has the potential both to free the listener from the weight of the word(s), and to interrupt the aural landscapes built with washes of captivating sounds. Wrote the Persian sage Jalaluddin Rumi: "Enough talking. If we eat too much greenery,/ we are going to smell like vegetables."[1]

Enough talking; and yet we go on talking and falling in love with green. We just can't stop. And I can't stop here, can I? With the media promotions of 'natural' products and imagery that saturate life in modern societies, it is difficult to continue putting nature back into discourse, without contributing to further denature nature by partaking in the production of its so-called "crisis"—or what a European critic views as a form of "intellectual blackmail[ing]" associated with that "epidemic of visibility menacing our entire culture."[2] At the end of the century, discourses on and images of nature seem to have taken on a new lease of life. With their proliferation, the concept of nature has at once regained its full importance and become so destabilized as to raise anew the question of its viability as a discursive category. In an attempt to introduce difference into practices that inform the theorizing of nature and to talk while not overeating greenery, a space is thus opened up here, in which reflections on nature necessarily shuttle between the arbitrary reality of the sign (word as word) and the multiple realities it speaks to or represents in the posthumanist landscapes of "denaturalized" discourses.

A few decades ago, Simone de Beauvoir wrote: "Nature is one of the realms [women] have most lovingly explored. For the young girl, . . . nature represents what woman herself represents for man: herself and her negation, a kingdom and a place of exile; the whole in the guise of the other . . . Few indeed there are who face nature in its nonhuman freedom, who attempt to decipher its foreign meanings, and who lose themselves in order to make union with this other presence."[3] *Herself and her negation*. The link between woman and nature is one that is at once constructed, capitalized on, and lovingly assumed. A look at the thinking conveyed in summer ads promoting feminine products and the new fragrances put out on the market in the nineties, suffices to confirm how thoroughly such a link continues to encode the natural. In the realm of the senses, for example, it is affirmed that the passion-driven imagery and the lusty scents of the eighties are definitely outdated. Today women are quoted saying they want to wear a scent for themselves, not necessarily for some men whom they want to attract or seduce. The focus is all on green. On the great outdoors, on fresh florals and on fruity scents. Green is definitely selling, and as remarked in a women's magazine, "the beauty biz has seen the future—and it's green, the very shade of a million-dollar bill!"

The world of media sensationalism has always proved to be very effective in its power of cooptation. It translates subversiveness into marketable pleasures and invests in the critical discourses that address the destruction of nature only so as to further work at raising up the green event for its mercantile purposes. Thus, partaking in the same historical network are both the discourses on nature that have been depicting it in terms of environmental crises and catastrophes, and those that continue to crown it in terms familiar to the tradition of taming and appropriating nature for the productions of culture. The slogan "green and clean," for example, has been readapted, as quoted earlier, to feminized contexts of pleasure, liberation and success, where images of the Garden of Eden, of the lost paradise, or of the forbidden fruit happily flourish. Like other cultural constructs, the concept of crisis is thereby always twofold: it constitutes a contestation of the despoiling of nature, at the same time as it gives a boost to the consumption of 'natural' products and of the environment. As a cultural critic cynically puts it, "together with mundane and operational eclecticism, crisis promotes all nostalgic and sentimental remakes from those of love to those of human rights, from those of fashion revivals to socialism in politics, and discourages everything regarded as adventurous."[4] *A kingdom and a place of exile.* The common tendency to oppose nature to culture, to feminize and primitivize it within the escalating logics of confine-and-conquer, or expropriate-and-dispossess systems fundamental to ideologies of expansionism, has been widely analyzed by feminists and postcolonial critics as part of a process of questioning the concepts of woman, otherness, and nature in relation to the globalizing projects of domination via (economic and cultural) modernization. Nature, the feminine and the primitive represented as the "no man's land" or the limit-zone of Man's symbolization, has undergone thorough scrutiny, and the critical debate has moved past the phases of assimilation and rejection to that of struggle (to use Frantz Fanon's terms), where affirmations and negations are diversely reappropriated as strategies and tactics toward the emergence of new subjectivities. Today, to come back to De Beauvoir's pessimistic statement, one would then have to turn its affirmation into a question: have there been, are there, indeed, so *few*—and who are they?—"who face nature in its nonhuman freedom . . . and lose themselves in order to make union with this other presence"?

Looking Back to the City of the Future

In Cheikh Amidou Kane's *Ambiguous Adventure*, the confrontation of a Frenchman (Paul Lacroix) and an African man of tradition ("the knight," or Samba Diallo's father) in the country of the Diallobe provides the reader with one of the novel's most remarkable scenes. Set at a time of the day when "on the horizon, it seemed as if the earth were poised on the edge of an abyss" above which "the sun was dangerously suspended," the scene invites reflection on the men's relationship with nature, as well as on the gap displayed between East and West, tradition and modernity, past and future. (After much resistance, Samba Diallo's father has here, finally, come to terms with the fact that his son will be sent to the new school and taught the values of the West, as required in the new system of government.)

    [Paul Lacroix] turned and spoke to him:
      "Does this twilight not trouble you? Myself I am upset by it. At this moment it seems to me that we are closer to the end of the world than we are to nightfall."

The knight smiled.

"Reassure yourself. I predict for you a peaceful night."

"You do not believe in the end of the world?"

"On the contrary, I even hope for it, firmly . . . Our world is that which believes in the end of the world: which at the same time hopes for it and fears it . . . from the bottom of my heart I wish for you to rediscover the feeling of anguish in the face of the dying sun. I ardently wish that for the West. When the sun dies, no scientific certainty should keep us from weeping for it, no rational evidence should keep us from asking that it be reborn. You are slowly dying under the weight of evidence . . . [Your science] makes you the masters of the external, but at the same time it exiles you there, more and more . . . M. Lacroix, I know that you do not believe in the shade; nor in the end of the world. What you do not see does not exist . . . The future citadel, thanks to my son, will open its wide windows on the abyss, from which will come great gusts of shadow upon our shriveled bodies, our haggard brows. With all my soul I wish for this opening. In the city which is being born such should be our work—all of us, Hindus, Chinese, South Americans, Negroes, Arabs, all of us."[5]

The fragile moment is that of a multiple encounter between day and night. As the sun goes dying in the west, the man of the East lets go of his mourning for the Diallobe that will go dying in his son's heart, and looks forward to the city of the future. In this moment, when ending and beginning mingle, and nothing seems evident to the eye and the ear, questions that arise remain dangerously suspended: is it the East or the West that is dying? What, exactly, is dying? As the tradition of the East gives way to the progress of the West, and as the West heads towards its own extinction under the weight of evidence, the world itself is coming to an end—the world as a concept for (implementing) a global society. The city of the future, as the African man has envisioned, is a city that is radically multiple as it can only survive in hope and fear, with its windows wide open onto the abyss.

"In the beginning was, *yesterday*, after which there has been many tomorrows,"[6] wrote Boubou Hama. The sight of the sunset in its full and dying splendor has never suscitated a uniform feeling among those whose relationship with nature is that of an intimate participant, rather than that of a spectator. The filmmaker Peter Kubelka, for whom it took a trip to a remote village in Africa to fully experience what he was trying for years to create in his films has, for example, the following event to relate back to his audience. When "it became evening," he wrote,

all attention was focused on the open plain. There was nothing to see but the people gathered to watch the plain and the horizon . . . then suddenly the drummers came and the excitement started to grow . . . the sun started to set, very fast . . . then exactly when the sun reached the horizon the chief made one bang on his drum. I was moved to tears because I saw my own motive right there . . . What I wanted to do with sound and light, they did too. This was a fantastic, beautiful sound sync event . . . This comparison of their sync event and mine exactly describes the situation of our civilization. Much less sensual substance and beauty, more speed. They had one day, I had every 24th of a second.[7]

Visual and aural, external and internal, passive and active at the same time, the sync event is evoked in Kubelka's context as a form of ecstasy, which he defines as a refusal to merely "serve time," to be a slave of nature, or to conform to the idealized cycle of life (birth, youth, age). Such an interpretation denotes a desire to defy the laws of nature—a desire particularly suited to the cinematic medium—but it also has the potential to introduce a break into the more familiar discourses of the West on its others, whose close relationship with nature continues to be depicted in terms of passive identification and submissive reverence. *There has been many tomorrows. Has been.* Here, the sync event is also a boundary event, for the moment when sight and sound meet is the very moment when the sun reaches the horizon—that is, when the curve and the straight line, the round and the flat, the circular and the linear seem to come into contact, and light starts mingling with darkness. "Every time the sun capsizes," wrote poet Jean-Joseph Rabearivelo, "he begins to suffer anew."[8] Anguish and ecstasy in the face of the dying sun. The feeling of the end of the world experienced anew every evening is widely conveyed in African literatures. A sunset is lived not necessarily and literally as the death of the sun, but as a rupture with and a continuation of the cycle of departing and returning. No real crisis. The "ambiguous adventure" is one in which the invasion of the evening awakens both fear and hope, and past and future are grasped in that moment of passage when "the known world was enriching itself by a birth that took place in mire and blood."[9] *Everything* is in the transition. (Or, there is no transition as suturing device.) Looking forward to the end of the world is also looking forward to a strange and terrible new dawn.

Boundary Event

In many Asian and African traditions the Western notion of "evil" as opposed to that of "good" remains largely unknown. For example, whenever the term devil is borrowed in the translation of *Kaydara*, an initiation text of the Fulani of the Niger Loop, it is said that it simply refers to one of the genii who work for the "supernatural spirits" and exercise their wits either to assist or to harass humans. They constitute a crowded population, which resides in what Amadou Hampâté Ba calls "the country of semi-darkness," and are subject to all kinds of incarnation. Such a country exists as an intermediary between "the country of light" where all species of the visible live, and "the country of profound night" where the souls of the dead and of those to-be-born from the human, the animal and the vegetal worlds are to be found.[10]

In Western cultures, the supernatural seems more easily locatable as it used to be confined to a genre known as the twilight tales. Associated with the world of ghosts and phantoms, of demonic and otherworldly beings, the supernatural is said to be always just around the corner. The mind that sees this other world as quite as real as, if not more so than, this world is called a "haunted mind." The technique, as a master of supernatural fiction writes, is to use the familiar and to "put the reader into the

position of saying to himself, 'If I'm not very careful, something of this kind may happen to me.'"[11] Thus, unlike in African literatures, where contact with the inhabitants of the countries of semi-darkness and of profound night is most likely initiated during a journey into the bush or beyond the boundaries of a settlement (of village life, of normal life), in many Western twilight tales the stage for the encounter with the supernatural is more often the haunted, abandoned house. Such a house, by "its apparent domesticity, its residue of family history and nostalgia, its role as the last and most intimate shelter of private comfort" which sharpens "by contrast the terror of invasion by alien spirits," has proven to be, since the nineteenth century, the most popular and "favored site for uncanny disturbances."[12]

On the one hand, reality is dichotomized, set into binary opposition, and dramatized in their contrast: domesticity-family-private comfort versus the invasion by demonic alien spirits; the invisible threatening to become visible; or the unfamiliar lurking in the midst of the most evidently familiar. On the other hand, reality is *set into motion* as it travels between the countries of light and of night, and shifts its boundaries as it moves from one marking, one territory, one light to another. Such a multi-dimensional fluidity has been hierarchized and explained by an observer of the West, Claude Lévi-Strauss, as follows:

> Among the peoples called "primitive," . . . the notion of nature always offers an ambiguous character. Nature is preculture and it is also subculture. But it is by and large the means through which man may hope to enter into contact with ancestors, spirits and gods. Thus, there is in the notion of nature a "supernatural" component, and this "supernature" is as undeniably above culture as nature itself is below it.[13]

Here, ambiguity offers a site where nature continues to resist hierarchized and linear categories. The prefixes pre-, sub-, and super- seem "hopelessly" irrelevant; so does the tendency incessantly to recenter "culture" and to revert to it as an organizing concept. After all, "If a ghost is seen . . . what sees it?" asked Algernon Blackwood, for whom our so-called normal waking consciousness is but one type of consciousness, by which only one person in a hundred is seen as "real."[14] What is unclear for the logic of rational knowledge may be crystal-clear for other forms of knowledge, and the "ambiguous character" of (the notion of) nature appears ambiguous only to those who refuse to participate in it. The haunted mind, the haunted house, the "real" person. Even when consciousness is extended to its outer limits, everything here seems to be confined to the precincts of humanist tradition. The anthropocentric overcast can seriously limit one's vision of things. Thus, returning to the West its own ethnocentric classifications Boubou Hama clears the field by specifying:

> Nothing in the universe is supernatural. Everything is natural. The supernatural is an anti-scientific invention of the West, its inability to grasp the spirit of matter and the soul of beings, and to distinguish the one and the other from the energy of matter.[15]

Twilight; two lights. Two countries; two worlds. It has always been difficult to determine where nature begins and where it ends. Especially when one recognizes oneself as being part of it. *Everything is natural. Spirit, soul, energy.* Realities change, for example, according to the shift of light, and meanings given to the same symbol may differ radically during daytime or nighttime. Again, in *Kaydara*, A. Hampâté Ba refers to knowledge of both cosmic order and disorder, of the annihilation of beings by other beings, and hence to the diurnal and nocturnal meanings encountered with each symbol. For example, among the seven attributes of the chameleon, "changing color, in the diurnal sense, is to be a sociable person . . . capable of maintaining good exchange with everyone, of adapting himself or herself to all circumstances . . . While in the nocturnal sense, the chameleon symbolizes hypocrisy . . . lack of originality and of personality."[16] Knowledge is, however, referred to here as being "far away and near by;" it is formless but does not hesitate to take on an adequate form when necessary, and the complexities of life are grasped, in both its binary and ternary symbols. Between the diurnal and the nocturnal, then, there is the third term; and there is a wide range of possible shades of meaning in the country of semi-darkness where all kind of incarnation is possible.

Indicative of the two extremes of a thing or an event, the third term carries with it the potential to change the term of every duality. In other words, it enables one to displace duality and reinscribe it as difference. An excerpt from Boubou Hama's novel, significantly titled *Le Double d'hier rencontre demain* (Yesterday's Double Meets Tomorrow), plays on the notion of "double" over that of duality in the following manner: "The dying evening marks the end of the world of he who is conditioned to live in full daylight; it is Souba's world in decline, while from its deepening shadow, emerges luminescent, the bright daylight of another world, the world of Bi Bio . . . Night, for him, is a 'blinding lighthouse'."[17] If supernature is contained within nature, if it only constitutes a site in which the forces of nature are humanized, if it is apprehended both within and beyond the boundaries of village life or culture; in other words, if night is lived within day, and day within night, then what is "natural" may be said to situate itself nowhere else than at the boundary of nature.

Nature's Becoming

The natural lies at the edge of nature and culture. Shifting from one realm, one context, one situation to another, its boundary challenges every definition of the 'natural' arrived at. Should writing be qualified as natural, then nature certainly proves to be writerly. "Music as I conceive it, is ecological . . . It IS ecology," wrote John Cage, who spoke of nature as a "together-work" of water, air, sky and earth—the separation of which (by humans) has put nature to danger.[18] Such a together work is what makes the difference between an art that imitates nature and one, as defined by Ananda K. Coomaraswamy, that "is like Nature, not in appearance, but in operation."[19] Realist art is here regarded as "decadent," for it is said to fall short of "what is proper to man as man, to whom not merely sensible, but also intelligible worlds are accessible," and hence, "the more an image is 'true to nature,' the more it lies."[20]

In the tradition of Asian arts, nature is always given a prominent role, but as a witness of events, or as a reality of its own, it is often not resorted to in mere metaphorical or

symbolical terms. Rather than simply reflecting the moods, the feelings or the states of mind of the writer or the onlooker, its function is more likely to *elicit* (these feelings and states) rather than to illustrate. It is known from the Sumiye School of painting, for example, that there could be no retouching whatsoever on a work, for the precise, swift and decisive brush strokes were effected on paper so thin that the slightest hesitancy would cause it to wrinkle and rend. Here the traces and gestures of painting are irrevocable, and the artistic work materializes a movement that depicts the becomingness of both nature and the human action-emotion-idea.

A boundary event. As such, painting is a form of comm-union with nature—or of natural responsibility/respond-ability—in the realm of no-knowledge. Born from silence, no-knowledge like no-thingness differs substantially from no knowledge and nothingness. The hyphen makes all the difference. Without it, the state of "infinite" sensibilities is both confused with the state of ignorance and reduced by narrow-minded rationalists to that of mystification. Nature *elicits* no-knowledge from the painter, and as R. G. H. Siu put it, "Creation in research is the fluorescence [/florescence] of no-knowledge."[21] In the state of becoming and un-becoming the thing known, a painting captures "the tigerishness of the tiger" and imparts what Siu considered to be "a feeling of nature that is rarely equaled in Occidental paintings with their anthropocentric overcast."[22] Su Tung-Po (1035–1101), whose influence among painters was widespread, suggested that in their works, emphasis be given not to exterior and fixed forms, but to grasping things in their becoming. What is thereby affirmed is the necessity to integrate vital Duration in painting. Li Jih-hua (1565–1635) further stressed the idea of such an internal transformation in theorizing the work of brush and ink as follows:

> In painting, it is important to know how to retain, but also how to let go . . . In the tracing of forms, although the goal is to fully reach a result, the entire art of execution resides in the intervals and the fragmentary suggestions. Hence the necessity to know how to let go. This implies that the painter's brush strokes interrupt themselves (without interruption of the breath that animates them) to better fill themselves with "surplus meaning." Thus, a mountain can comprise unpainted sections and a tree can do without parts of its branches in such a manner that these remain, in this state of becoming, between being and non-being.[23]

A duration event. Partaking in nature's manner of operation, the painting can be said to be a becoming-nature/becoming-culture/becoming-human. What breathes through Li Ji-hua's intervals, what governs the absences-presences or centers-absences, what moves in the space-between is not the missed, hidden or impenetrable thing, but rather, the no-thing becoming (the thing) not-quite-not-yet known. Shen-Hao (seventeenth century), whose treatise on painting insisted on the necessity of taking inspiration directly from nature, related that after having been inspired one night to paint bamboo according to the *i* (translated as idea, desire, intention, acting conscience, accurate vision), the painter Ni Yu discovered upon waking up the next morning that his painted bamboo differed wildly from the real ones, and exclaimed laughingly: "To resemble nothing, but that's exactly what's most difficult!"[24] Night-into-day realizations, like all work carried out in frontier realms, have at all times been a challenge to artists and writers. As Ch'ien Wen-shih (from the Sung Dynasty, 960–1279) had specifically noted:

> It is easy to paint a mountain in clear or rainy weather. But how far more difficult it is to grasp this state between being and non-being, when the fine weather is about to give way to the rain, or inversely, when the rain begins to clear and to yield to the fine weather. Or else, when bathed in the morning mists or in the sunset smokes, things immersed in semi-darkness are still distinct, but they are already nimbed by an invisible halo that unites them all.[25]

At the edge of. Rather than being a spectator of nature, the painting subject enters becomings-nature. The first of the six canons formulated by Hsieh Ho (sixth century) asserted that the work of art must reveal "the operation of the [breath/] spirit (ch'i) in life movement."[26] In a painting without *ch'i*, the forms are, indeed, said to be lifeless. Wang Wei (699–759) held that, as with the I-Ching and its ever-moving lines, paintings in their language of brush, form and symbol, should inscribe the ever-changing processes of nature. Shih T'ao (1641–after 1710) further advocated the art of probing the "unforeseeable mutations" of the Landscape, while Pu Yen-t'u (eighteenth century) wrote about the necessity of integrating the infinite in the finite, the invisible in the visible, for "all elements of nature which appear finite are in reality linked to the infinite."[27] A multitude of examples could be cited here of other traditional Asian painters whose practices, rather than seeking resemblance with nature's outward appearance (hsing), involve the movement of its becomingness.

Of no less relevance in the leap from tradition to postmodernity, and from East to West, are the names of contemporary theorists like Gilles Deleuze and Felix Guattari. The latter may be said to have come very close to "Oriental mysticism" and to have been particularly stimulated by the so-called inscrutable Asian aesthetic experience of "union with nature," when they expand on the rhizome as "all manner of 'becomings'." On binary logic and the One-becomes-Two law that dominates Western classical thought, Deleuze and Guattari remark: "Nature doesn't work that way; in nature, roots are taproots with a more multiple, lateral, and circular system of ramification, rather than a dichotomous one." To the Western model of the tree-root and its centralized, hierarchical arborescent systems, they oppose the Eastern model of the rhizome, which cannot be reduced either to the One or to the multiple derived from the One, and "is composed not of units but of . . . *directions in motions.*"[28]

A becoming is not a resemblance, an imitation, identification or an evolution by descent. It creates nothing other than itself since its order is never that of filiation but of alliance. Thus, becoming always involves at least a double movement, for what one becomes also becomes: "The painter and musician do not imitate the animal, they become-animal at the same time as the animal becomes what they willed, at the deepest level of their concord with Nature."[29] Deleuze and Guattari further designate the rhizome as being made of plateaus and located "in the middle, between things, interbeing, *intermezzo*": having no culmination or termination points, its movement is that of coming and going, rather than of starting and finishing. The middle is "by no means an average . . . *Between* things does not designate a localizable relation going from one thing to the other and back again, but . . . a stream without beginning or end that undermines its banks and picks up speed in the middle."[30]

Here, one is easily reminded of the concept of the Middle Ground or the Median Way in Chinese theories of art and knowledge. Middleness in this context does not refer to a static center, nor does it imply any compromise or lack of determination. A median position, on the contrary, is where extremes lose their power; where all directions are (still) possible; and hence, where one can assume with intensity one's freedom of movement. As such, it is a place of decentralization that gives in to neither side, takes into its realm the vibrations of both, requiring thereby constant acknowledgment of and transformation in shifting conditions. Middleness (Chung) is usually paired with (what has been translated as) Harmony (Ho). Here again, harmony does not connote uniformity: it is "a multitude and diversity of notes and motions . . . Harmony is not only compatible with differences but without them there can be no harmony."[31] Difference is thus paired with harmony, rather than with conflict. (Difference has too often been pointed to as the cause and the source of conflict, whereas difference may be said to exist without, within and alongside conflict.) A harmony-difference-middleness. To return to Deleuze and Guattari's terms, what is designated in this space between the extremes is not a localizable relation or a mere shuttling between two recognizable points, but "a perpendicular direction, a transversal movement that sweeps one *and* the other way."[32]

Twilight Gray, Middle Gray

It is known that the Western notion of *nature morte* in art does not really exist in the traditional conception of painting in the Far East. Indeed, it matters little whether a flower, a fruit or a whole landscape is drawn, for even when a single bamboo is materialized, what is depicted and seen by the beholder is a grove of bamboos in its density, or further still, Nature itself in its vastness.[33] To seize the ch'i (life breath/spirit) that animates the bamboo and to let it draw its own inner form on paper or on silk is to actualize a whole landscape in its motions, multiplicities and alliances. Awareness of the becoming space between being and non-being and of the principle of expression through non-expression prevails in the aesthetic and spiritual consciousness of the East. As Siu noted, "The Indian Samkara maintains that in observing things we not only perceive our perceptions but something which is neither ourselves nor our perceptions."[34]

In classic Japanese literature, nature is often equated with color. To go toward nature is to encounter color. Nature's infinitely varied colors can intoxicate one's aesthetic sense. Widely referred to as a place of spiritual repose, it offers the contemplative onlooker a beauty both to be dazzled by and to meditate upon—in other words, a beauty that inevitably goes on changing with the moments of the day and the seasons of the year, whether it is cherished in its sumptuous tones or in its subdued shades. The ancient word for "color," iro, is thus said to evoke "the idea of time passing, of change with its multifold meanings . . . In its nuance of 'beautiful' hues iro instantly suggests beauty that fades or feelings that are inconstant." It came to mean "woman, prostitute, or lover as the [passing] object of [man's] desire."[35] Nature, color(s), woman, sex. Nature, spirit, shade(s), repose. Conjuring up a familiar image of Nature, these two sets of combined realities do not really stand in opposition to one another; they are simply two of the possible and existing multiplicities woven here by a thread that links the process of "reviving" to that of "killing" Color/Nature.

Nature: the feminine, the sexual, but also the supernatural, the spiritual. The Rest. A poem (by Teika Fugiwara, 1162–1241) constantly quoted by the tea-men as their motto reads:

> All around, no flowers in bloom are seen,
> Nor blazing maple leaves I see,
> Only a solitary fisherman's hut I see,
> On the sea beach, in the twilight of this autumn eve.[36]

A beauty that fades; a feeling that wavers between nostalgia and unqualifiable lucidity (*not seen/I see*); a reaching out in unforeseen directions toward outer circles named 'past,' 'future,' or 'unspecified present;' or else, a situating at the boundary of natural and supernatural thought, apparent and real in-existences. The end-of-the-world image offered above is again that of a twilight moment—a becoming-no-thing moment—in which the play on the visible and the invisible creates a sense of intense ephemeral reality approaching spiritual absoluteness. The supernatural is always right around the corner. It is the all-too-tangible presence of an absence within the natural. Faithful to the tradition of Far Eastern aesthetic, the poem offers a perception of nature *in the course of change*. It depicts the interstate of being and non-being via the presence and absence of color/nature. What is explicitly pointed to in the verses as a lack or a deficiency is actually what allows the monochrome landscape to reach its "supreme beauty." Brilliant colors are thus positively presenced in the negative (*no*, *nor*), via a chromatic restraint. They are brought to the reader's vision only to lead the latter to the colorless color of the fisherman's hut standing by itself on the sea beach in the twilight gray of the autumn evening.

The tea-men's poem is an example of "artistic asceticism," "chromatic reticence" and "remarkable natural inclination . . . toward the subdual or suppression of color" that Toshihiko Izutsu considers to be revealing of "one of the most fundamental aspects of Far Eastern culture."[37] Such an "aesthetic consciousness" does not result from a lack of appreciation for color; on the contrary, it has grown out of a context of highly refined sensibility for color and for the infinite subtleties of its hues. For example, the writings of court women that constituted the prose of the Heian period (794–1185) mentioned the names of more than 170 different colors, all to be elaborately combined into color harmonies (such as in the art of clothing and costuming). Differentiated from this period of aristocratic aesthetic refinement that is said to verge on "effeminacy" is the Momoyama period (1573–1615), permeated with "virile vitality," a period during which the Japanese taste for dazzlingly brilliant colors and exuberant decorations reached its second peak. Yet, alongside the world of refined and vivid colors of these periods also existed the totally different world of black-and-white painting, or rather, of vaporous-gray and spared-ink painting attributed to the impact of Zen Buddhism (which thrived during the Kamakura period [1192–1333] and produced masterpieces of monochrome painting during the Muromachi period [1392–1573]). Thus, the taste for the extravagant display of color during the Momoyama period went hand in hand with the distaste for colorful show—an aesthetic chromatic reticence that linked the pictorial art to the art of tea, via the teaching of Tea-Master Sen no Rikyu, also known as Soeki (1521–1591).[38]

Among the instructions Soeki gave to practitioners of the art of tea was that of wearing "cotton kimono dyed with ash to a neutral hue." As is well known, the master's advocation of simplicity and restraint achieved a widespread following, and with the art of tea gaining ground, the color gray grew so popular among the people that Japan came to be culturally associated with the "ash-dyed neutral hue," the "rat color," or twilight color of Rikyu gray. A wide range of shades of gray obtained through the matting and subduing of colors dominated Japanese aesthetic sensibility from the Genroku era (1688–1704) to the Tenmei era (1781–1789) and beyond. The contemporary architect and theorist Kisho Kurokawa, for example, does not hesitate to refer to all of Japanese culture as to "a culture of grays" when he proceeds to define its spatial character and open-ended aesthetic. Seeing in Rikyu gray a colorless color of numerous hues that collide, neutralize, and hence cancel each other out, Kurokawa further claims it as his personal label for the multiple meanings and simultaneous possibilities of things. He writes:

> Rikyu gray works to transform volumetric, sculptural, physical space into planar, pictorial space. The streets of Tokyo, and indeed of all traditional Japanese towns in general, take on a special beauty in the graying light of dusk. There is a fusing of perspectives as the slate-colored tiles and white plaster walls dissolve into gray, flattening all sense of distance and volume; a drama of transition from three-dimensions down to two which is not often seen in Western cities.[39]

Such a sense of two-dimensionality is said to lie at the heart of all creative manifestations of traditional Japanese culture, whether in painting, theater, music, architecture or city design. Kurokawa further names "gray space," the intervening area between inside and outside and a realm where both the interior and the exterior merge. He describes as the "gray zone in time" the concept of *senuhima* or "undone interval" of pause, which was developed by Zeami Motokiyo (1364?–1443) to designate the moment of suspended action and of "no mind" in the art of Noh drama. Among the many other terms that speak of the temporal, physical or spiritual "gray" quality of Japanese culture, he also mentions the word *ne* which is used for musical sounds created both by man and in nature. "It stands," he remarks, "midway between sound and music—representing the gray space between these two realms. Again the concept of *ne* embodies the Japanese inclination to recognize, live with and preserve continuity with nature."[40]

The Faded Charm of the Wolf

A drama of transition. A beauty that fades. The lures of decline, of passing things and of the past. Nature is never static, and *music is ecology.* In color genetics, gray is said to be at the center of humans' sphere of colors. A human is thus gray in the midst of the chromatic world. But plain gray as defined earlier in Japanese aesthetics is not so much the result of a mixing of equal parts of black and white as it is "the color of no color" in which all colors are canceling each other out. The new hue is a distinct color of its own, neither black nor white, but somewhere in between—in the middle where possibilities are boundless. *Intermezzo.* A midway-between-color, gray is composed of multiplicities, or to borrow Deleuze and Guattari's terms, of "directions in motions." As Kurokawa specifies, "in contrast to grey in the West, which is a combination of white and black, Rikyu grey was a combination of four opposing colors: red, blue, yellow and white."[41]

Rikyu gray is a manner of becoming. A becoming-no/color. The temporal, physical and mental interval between two phenomena takes on here a compelling visual (pictorial, painterly, non-realist-two-dimensional), musical and spiritual dimension. Without this dimension, gray remains largely (in Japanese as well as in many Western contexts) a dull color within culture's boundaries: one that usually implies a lack of brightness; an unfinished state; a dreary and spiritless outlook (the gray prospects, the gray office routine); a negative intermediate condition or position (that evades, for example, the spirit of moral and legal control without being overtly immoral and illegal); sadness, melancholia, boredom, unpleasantness (gray weather, *faire grise mine*); and last but not least, the polluting of the natural world by ecologically destructive technology (in which modern Japan partakes as one of the most powerful producers). *Much less sensual substance and beauty, more speed.* Developing a relationship to nature mediated through machines made to dominate nature paradoxically means nurturing nostalgia for nature not yet tamed for humans' utilitarian purposes. *Nature, color, woman, sex.*

The ecofeminist critique of the natural and social sciences has shown that fulfillment of this modernized desire for wilderness is often satisfied by adventure tourism and sex tourism (such as in Thailand, Kenya, the Dominican Republic). American, European, and Japanese business men travel around the globe to have sexual experience with, if not to acquire, an exotic "passing beauty"—a temporary and "inconstant" object of desire—that resides in or comes from the remote parts of the under- or non-industrialized world. The further from the (men's) mind and the closer to nature the object of desire acquired abroad is, the more likely it is to provide compensation for these men's alienation from nature in their culture. It is as if the sexual act has become virtually the only direct contact to nature available to the man of modern technology; "a sexual act which becomes itself entangled in the net of consumption and economic exploitation, or which becomes the sacred refuge, outside ordinary life."[42]

A becoming-exploitation, a becoming-refuge. The sexual and the spiritual both have their share in nature. *Between the extremes . . . is a perpendicular direction, a transversal movement that sweeps one and the other way.* Between the countries of light and of night is the country of semi-darkness whose inhabitants travel in the diurnal *and* nocturnal meanings of things, passing from one incarnation to another, turning into . . . In Christian symbolics, gray designates the *resurrection of the dead.* Artists in the Middle Ages painted Christ's coat gray—the color of ash and of fog—when he presided at the last judgment. Here, to cover oneself with ashes is to express intense pain, for ash-gray is the color of half-mourning. Evoking dreams that appear in grayish fog is also to situate them in the layers of the unconscious, in the process of emerging into consciousness (doesn't the French expression *se griser,* or to be half-drunk, resort to gray as a color of semi-consciousness?). One can say that the fog is a transcultural symbol of that which is indeterminate ("the gray area"); it indicates a phase of (r) evolution, between form and formlessness, when old forms are disappearing while new ones coming into view are not yet distinguishable.

In Far Eastern paintings, for example, horizontal and vertical fogs constitute a disturbance in the unfolding of the narrative, a transition in time, a passage to the supernatural, a transitory period between two states of things and a prelude to manifestation.[43]

The delicate, diffused, ephemeral and transitory lights of dawn and dusk have always been the lights most sought after in color photography. It is, indeed, during the "magic hours" of sunrise and sunset that photographers fully capture the muted hues and subtleties of tone that appear with the gradual deepening and fading of colors. Just as poets are attracted to changeability and to the recurring act of becoming, photographers are drawn to the swift transformations effected with the shifting early morning and evening lights. Fascinated by the frail sunlight that penetrates the morning mist, John Hedgecoe, for example, remarks: "Minute by minute, a world composed entirely of tones of gray is tinted until colors intensify and glow even in the angular shadows."[44] He further notes that the dimmer light of dusk is best for photographing wildlife, for not only are saturated colors achievable in late light, but nocturnal animals begin to emerge in search for food . . . *Dissolve into gray, flattening all sense of distance and volume.* Dusk is also the spatio-temporal image of the suspended instant, "a drama of transition" in which maintaining definition over the whole of the subject is quasi impossible, for the low light demands a wide aperture which means a shallow depth of field. *Every time the sun capsizes, he begins to suffer anew.* Twilight: the hours of melancholia, loss and nostalgia; but also of preparation for a renewal, when the sun sets in the west, the moon rises in the east, and the ending passes into the beginning. The journey to the west is, no doubt, the journey toward the future, through dark transformations.

Needless to say, the hope for and the fear of the end of the world, the powerful and peaceful experience of twilight as the coming and going of color, the waning and waxing of desire, or the ability to open wide into the abyss of the world of shadows, constitute a site where East and West both depart and meet—literally, literarily. One of the most striking passages in *Un Captif amoureux* is, for example, the passage in which Jean Genet related his erotic and political relationship with Palestinian soldiers while casting what he saw as the *flamboyance* of their struggle and physical appeal in the *gray* tones of twilight:

> the expression *entre chien et loup* (literally, between dog and wolf, that is dusk, when the two can't be distinguished from each another) suggests a lot of other things besides the time of the day. The color grey, for instance, and the hour when night approaches as inexorably as sleep, whether daily or eternal. The hour when street lamps are lit in the city . . . The hour in which—and it's a space rather than a time—every being becomes his own shadow, and thus something other than himself. The hour of metamorphoses, when people half hope, half fear that a dog will become a wolf. The hour that comes down to us from at least as far back as the Middles Ages, when country people believed that transformation might happen at any moment.[45]

Genet's above description of dusk uncannily reminds one of the previously quoted conversation between the African man of tradition and the French man of modernity in Cheikh Amidou Kane's *Ambiguous Adventure*. Similar terms are used to depict the "inconstant feeling" (half hope, half fear; becoming-shadow; the peacefulness of sleep and the anxiety of transformation) that arises when the sun capsizes. For contemporary Westerners and city dwellers, Genet specified: the expression *entre chien et loup* "has a certain faded charm, because . . . we don't know much about wolves now, and no one believes any more that a dog might turn into one." But for Genet himself, in the Middle East, rather than connoting twilight, the expression "describes any, perhaps all, of the moments of a *fedayee's* life."[46]

In today's need to return to nature and to theorize it anew, one can say that the rejection of all that is romantic and nostalgic strives with a strong attraction to all that is declining and ending, and their strange ecstasies. The "adventure" is an "ambiguous" one whose effortless radiance is at once sweet and strong, hopeful in its hopelessness. It is by listening to the evening, to the fading sounds of this moment of multiplicities, transformations and metamorphoses that one's ears open up to the sight of two worlds wavering across the sky. Such a sight has its own becoming-sound story; one which Kubelka, moved to tears and in ecstasy, calls a one-day sound sync event; and one also in which nature's r is here read specifically as a middle ground and, . . . *a musical swoon*. For between sound and sense, if rhythm isn't, then writing/nature isn't either. One never stops listening to the tone, timbre and rhythm of words. And when nature is heard as nonsense, (its) music will sound through, unhampered. Again, nature will be heard.

Voice Over I

First published in *Talking With Your Mouth Full*, ed. Steve
Fagin (Durham: Duke University Press, 1998), pp. 261–66. The
piece was written in relation to the voice-over that I performed,
as one of the narrators for Fagin's video, *The Machine That
Killed Bad People* (120 minutes, 1990).

Air (YOUR TONGUE)

And sensuality? Sensuality follows the listeners. For some, it delights, moves, awakens
desire; for others, it sows doubt, irritates, and is finally rejected on the side of femininity.

From the depths of . . ., on the very surface, it tells all my secrets. I can't hear it
without feeling exposed. Whose is it?

A voice. Over. I.

Voice: in the confines of this relationship with the body, from the inside out, between
absence and presence, desire. The voice of the name appearing on the image is a fiction.
The speaker, the news reporter, or the narrator has a fictive identity, for I is a fiction
of identity. Not all of what is seen, heard, smelled, tasted and felt is representable, for
I represent not I. I read what I've been told and all of a sudden, I hear my own voice.
I am (no) other than the eye I represent, or the represented I. The tongue that falsifies
must then be trimmed, cut, edited. Selectively staged. Tactically turned over. Dis-played
aloud, always interrupted in its breath. A site of love, a tear on silence. Voice evokes
rape. Unapproachable, it arouses sexual desires. Does it lie? No, identity and non-identity
meet in the question asked; they interact in the same sound space. Perhaps it is too
difficult to find the word in which it lies, and one goes on wondering which I in the
impassioned eye? An I that reads, an I that hears, or an I you hear? What asserts itself
over the eye, the image, the non-displayed silence would have to be both an absent
presence and a present absence. The eye/I reading is finally more I than the I saying I.

A voice exists in voicing. On its materiality—physical, erotic, *and* uninhabitable—a
world is being built in the projected intervals of image, words, music, and silence.
Likely to suscitate disappointment and disgust is the ease with which one summarizes,
explains, classifies, assimilates, neutralizes, impersonalizes, hence co-opts and destroys.
Beg-in a-gain. I hear myself detached from myself in the space of sound time. There,

something is uttered that has no head no tail, and with each word emitted, I perceive myself faltering, sickened by the sound taking shape in the hollow of my throat. My, mine; often moved by an urgent desire, not so much to deform the world becoming sound becoming form through such a closed venue, as to simply let free. If only the words can (be let) ring or die. They can swell, I can make my body resonate, and perhaps inscribe: here one does not speak; one groans, moans, sighs; one breathes. Resists. Turns faint, inaudible. Lovers becoming sound becoming animals are so much alike. There is no longer I, but only Sighs, Sighs, Moans, Moans, Breaths. Nothing original, nothing personal, yet all intensely intimate. The unique, irreplaceably non-personal intimacy. Here, one can only gasp for Air as one finds one's way through the long, stuffy, densely packed corridor of intentional meaning.

Move your tongue over your lips.

Earth (YOUR LIPS)

Voice has no memory. Free of context and of development, it reads blindly, understanding "everything of what others read but nothing of what it reads" (to quote myself quoted). I is always past. The eye of the voice is an absent eye, not yet subject nor quite object. In my own voice, I would stray away from meaning. Voice would slip into non-sense, coming closer to the scream, the laugh, the cry, the song. The onomatopoeias of a loving body. It caresses, makes desire audible. Voice then, not in the words, but in their sounds, in the way it sounds and sculpts the space it traverses. A half-audible, half-silenced movement of lust, thirst and hunger is projected, captured, to reveal not what cannot be seen, or what remains absent, but what seems not to lend itself to representation. Loving. When the non-representable finds its place in the relation of word, sound, silence and image, or of timbre, tone, dynamics and duration, meaning can only circulate at the limit of sense and non-sense.

One goes on hearing, eyes shut. Loses one's breath, as time seems to come to a standstill. Here, where air is rarefied . . . A swoon. All lights become dimmers. Insight, intuition and other sensorial faculties let go of their ingenuity, leaving room for an overfocused in-. Intensity. Less and less clear as the lips touch each other, less and less sharp as the sounds roll out, deformed in their contours, barely recognizable, and above all not-yet-not-quite finished. The voice keeps on drifting, incomplete, continually growing and coming into being, stretching beyond sense, beyond sight, beyond pleasure, toward uncertainty and undesirability, toward its own peril. Own death. Breath.

A present without presence. A voice (re) recorded. A loss of subjectivity. What if what one hears as "true," "authentic," "personal" is nothing other than a ghostly projection, a dis-embodied sound of a body in love with its own sound? Swallow and wet your lips. As meaning enters and settles down, beware, voice becomes conscious of its "significance," its role as holder of truth and of knowledge. Voice becomes Someone's voice. It centers. Carries a specific function, for it is there to inform, to state "facts," to *cover* the news, to give mean-ing to non- and not-yet-mean-ingful events. It fulfills its useful task and becomes *voice* all *over* again. Overtly situated, *covertly* omniscient. Or is it the other way around? What makes it ring off-site? Oddly enough, what seems strange is when it sounds true. No doubt, it's all wet.

Water (YOUR SALIVA)

And sensuality. Can anything sound drier? More senseless? S-wallow, clear y-our throat. The spit lands on the sidewalk, on the floor in a restaurant, on the train, in a bus, neatly next to one's foot between two seats in a movie theater. It hardly *looks* inspiring. And yet . . . Constantly darting and licking, the tongue continues its favorite activity, wetting the entire skin surface of the lips, cheeks, chin and throat. Do you care for more (water)? Again, I insist: and sensuality? Your parched lips. Always in want of the moist that refuses to dwell, or spread. Sensuality doesn't belong to the visible or to the audible, it hardly articulates. It caresses. Sometimes one hears it too well; it overwhelms. Other times one solicits it in vain. It remains absent, barely there, already somewhere else. When it comes, it goes; it returns weeks after, unexpectedly. Creating a resonance more subtle than sound, more persistent than sight, it is a physics of the voice, comparable in precision and in intensity to the infinity of pentamerous rhythm.

Streams and rivers held internally are released and externalized in gradients. The voice heard is an aural glyph for the inner experience of pitch, volume and rhythm. Without practice, it is easily silted over. One would then have to wash it clean to make it resonate anew. A waking up to sound and voice can open to an intimate love for the basic creative elements of music and the primary directions of creation—north, south, east, west, and the Middle or the empty center. Of the five intoxications to which one easily falls prey, as they say in many parts of Asia, music is the fifth, the four others being beauty, wealth, power, and knowledge. Music is both the source of creativity and the means to receive it. Your saliva heals and destroys. Gives life and dissolves it. Engenders, regenerates, moistens, softens, or insults. Certainly it arouses and calms, awakens or kills desire. The passion, the art of transmitting saliva. The science and the eroticism of breath. The violence-becoming-tenderness of that movement without memory between receptivity (in creation) and creativity (in reception). Attraction and repulsion are, in the end, all music.

Light (THE WAY YOU MOVE)

Voice structures both physical and narrative space. With it, desire is made audible, rhythmic. Breath is manifested as word, as sound, as music, and silence is reintroduced into the image. The voice renders, it doesn't reproduce. It works as a sound seer whose rhythms translate less the realities evoked than the internal life of its own constitutive elements. Here, one is bound to read blindly. Or to go blind while hearing oneself speaking. The timbre, tone and rhythm can enliven myriads of sensations—visual, tactile, spatial, temporal. Can you see it?

Some viewers-listeners never really cross these thresholds, who conceive the voice only as information and communication. They do not hear. Have heard nothing. Caught in de-ci-phering rather than in re-ceiving, they find meaning in the said, the all-too-visible. They? I. I too listen to myself speaking meaningfully when I set out to represent (an) other voices. And I may forget a moment of no meaning; no understanding does not necessarily hinder understanding. The two, as Dogen reminds, are like spring and autumn. In love with one another. Since the sky in its entirety lies in a drop of water, it is often not in front of images that one dreams. One encounters a voice and embarks

on a journey of no return. One hears it before one even becomes a spectator-listener. A voyage is produced not by the vision or the sound projected, but by a musical receptivity that allows one to tune in before the event, toward the softness of a becoming-voice—a spirit in motions. In this twilight reverie, the ear is led, between sense and sound, from "non-formed" to not-yet-formed words, from hints of articulation to hints of inarticulation, from silent cues to half-said, half-sung vowels and consonants. And the journey continues its course, exposing itself as site of transience and availability, as play between rupture and rapture.

The complex harmonies make the voice hang in the image space, which remains suspended in what it shows and says. A long tone, for example, is not a boring one-line-event, but a multiplicity of moments shifting wildly between the raw and the cooked. That darkness in voicing: an odor of bodily liquid, the fragrance of a familiar breath. Melody loses its central role when pleasure comes with the ability to travel through different tonal places, to render a timbre in its fullness, or to explore the dynamics of overtones. Sensitivity to timbre and tone, over- and under-, keeps one alert to the subtlest changes of light and color, shades and hues. The tones with which you speak are so many seeds disseminated in the space through which you move.

Finally, one never stops listening to the rhythm of a voice, whether consciously or unconsciously. If the rhythm doesn't work, the voice doesn't work. Nothing comes together; nothing comes apart; only the stagnancy and monotony of a spiritless utterance lend themselves to one's reading and hearing. There are as many voices as there are "souls," it is often said. One may be born to a certain pitch, a certain tone and a certain timbre, but what is "natural" becomes "magical" when, in the manner of nature, it is developed and cultivated. Perhaps, to practice the erotic science of breath is to learn how to perform simple activities such as: to make a sound, to say a word, to pause, to be silent. In other words, to let one's breath find its rhythm, to let one's voice find its way. Powerful in its vulnerability. Magical in its simplicity.

The Paint of Music
A Performance across Cultures

First published in *Writings on Dance* (Australia), Vol. 13 (Autumn, 1995).

Art lies in the slender margin between the real and the unreal
—Chikamatsu Monzaemon

The name is the performance. Theater, dance, mime, art, architecture, music, film, video, other. What is born from the combination and at the intersection of different idioms continues to defy naming. The easier the distinctions between genres and categories, the smaller the capacity to depart from and return to performance as a (in) finite spectacle. Art situated both outside and inside "art" loses its fixed boundaries. As a (named) message it palls, passes, and perishes. As a (naming) sign, it is the work of rhythm: breath manifested as voice, body, space. Or sound, movement, light: the vibration of a gesture—from silence; the resonance of space—from darkness; the music of life—from stillness. The "frame" is the performance. It takes form by limiting, yet its finality remains free of attachment to an end. The same critical work of naming and framing arrests the flow from outside-in-inside-out and incites movement across (the) borders (of the frame). What has come to perfection perishes. Without the potential for new departures and returns, its vitality is doomed to wane with the rivalry of that other measure of perfection named: imperfection.

Essence—Performance

In the art of Japanese Noh theater, master Zeami Motokiyo (also spelled Seami, 1363–1443) identified three aspects of the art and equated them with the senses: seeing was called the skin, hearing the flesh, and feeling the bones. While failing to find anyone among his contemporaries who could offer more than "a feeble representation of just the skin," he insisted that performers not only possess all three qualities, but also develop these qualities to their limits. The performance, in other words, should be "effortless and ineffable."[1]

Truth requires the most imagination. "True accomplishment" cannot be attained merely through the assiduous search for it or the accumulated efforts to materialize it. Those who only see with their eyes are said to see only the performance, which they seek to imitate. But, wrote actor and theorist Zeami, there is no such thing as performance by itself, for without the "essence" there cannot be any "performance." The relation between the two is compared to that of a flower and its fragrance, or the moon and the light it sheds. "To imitate the performance is to create a false essence"—one "doomed eventually to perish."[2] Here, imitation of the false means both limitation and lack: the inability to go beyond the limit of one's immediate perception, and to accomplish the arts of the flesh and the bones. Truth, apparently, does not yield itself to what is shown or said. One may grasp it as event, never really as substance. Didn't the poet Basho (1644–1694) already warn: "Do not seek to follow in the footsteps of the men of the old; seek what they sought"?[3]

What one calls the "truth" of a performance is a form of language among others. Since each language carries with it a certain mental context and a locatable history of thought, to read "essence" across contextual borders, one must necessarily displace it from the central position it occupies within Western metaphysics. Founded on the notion of pure (self-) presence—Being as full presence, absolute proximity to oneself, or nondifference—such metaphysics moralizes according to its humanistic tradition and its own idea of True and False, Good and Evil. Thus, "essence" in Zeami's writings requires a multiple, different/differing reading. The relation it establishes with performance is not so much that of a mere opposition between true and false, as that of a mutual challenge between change and permanence, the two vital principles of life and art. "If you must make spasmodic effort to search for it and, having found it, to hold it up ostentatiously," Polish drama teacher Jerzy Grotowski also remarked, "then the tradition is no longer alive inside you. There is no point to do that which has ceased to be alive because it will not be true."[4] Here, what changes and cannot be merely held up to view is alive; what is no longer alive is not true; and what is true presents itself effortlessly, for what usually takes shape independently of effort lies at the limits of the performable and the expressible.

A Musical Accuracy

Zeami's pairing of essence and performance calls into mind the mindful mindlessness of both Basho's *haikai* and Merce Cunningham's dances. Excelling in a verse-form that may be best described as an awakening to the thing in its fragile essence of appearance, Basho noted, for example, that: "A good poet does not 'make' a poem; he keeps contemplating his subject until it becomes a poem."[5] While he carried on the tradition of Japanese literary criticism, evaluating the merit of a poem according to the proportion of "surplus meaning" (*yojo*) it offers, Basho also insisted that there be no predecessors in the poetry of his school, and that both change and permanence be the essence of *haikai*. What makes this verse-form a major contribution to the poetic literature of the world is apparently its unpretentiousness. *Hakai* poetry has been evolved for the ordinary man and woman, and historically it allowed Japanese poets to break with what used to be the incontestable measure of perfection: the conventional aristocratic practice of imitating the masterpieces of their predecessors and of restricting themselves to the same vocabulary. Thus, it is hardly surprising that Basho, who made *haikai* the glory of the Japanese people and whose poetry (partly due to the attention it gave to the humor of the everyday details of our lives) has become popular with people of every class, also be the man who declared in his time: "My poetry is like a stove in the summer or a fan in winter. It runs against the popular tastes and has no practical use."[6]

The story of poetess Chiyo (1703–1775) is another well-known example of poetic performance as "becoming" rather than "making." In her quest for what constituted a genuine *haiku* and her eagerness to widen the local fame she had already acquired, she met with a noted *haiku* master who happened to visit her town. He then asked her to compose a poem about a conventional subject: the cuckoo. One of the favorite birds of Japanese *haiku* poets, the cuckoo distinguishes itself in that it sings in the night as it flies, making it difficult for the observer to translate its fleeting visual or aural presence. Chiyo tried, but again and again the master rejected every one of her attempts as being "not true to feeling." One night, as related by Daisetz T. Suzuki, while losing herself intently in the subject, she failed to notice the day already dawning through the paper screens, "when the following *haiku* formed itself in her mind":

> Calling "cuckoo," "cuckooo,"
> All night long
> Dawn at last!

Upon its reading, the master at once decreed it to be one of the finest *haiku* ever composed on the cuckoo.[7] A most conventional subject thus takes on a new lease of life as the unique moment it offers is also a most banal, "true-to-feeling" moment in which criteria based on "popular taste" and "practical use" turn out to be essentially inappropriate.

In the state of "no-mind"/Noh mind, the highly mystified "presence" of the artist is both a presence and an absence to one-self. The moment in and out of time is the movement outside of the self—in itself. Chiyo's most "genuine" *haiku* materializes a state of becoming speech in which neither the inside nor the outside is privileged. What is achieved is not exactly the "ineffable," but a musical accuracy—an "echoless breach of meaning," as Roland Barthes put it,[8] for the music referred to here is both a music of meanings and a music of sounds. The awakening to "the suchness of thing" has no ulterior motive. It is, as Suzuki put it in Christian terms, "to see God in a flea as a flea."[9]

Merce Cunningham's dances, for example, also express nothing but themselves. Instead of telling a story or exploring the relationship between movement and the psyche, they focus on the physicalness of the body. In other words, they feature the body simply as "a way of moving." Cunningham composes movement with no attempts to direct expressivity, and with no specific meaning or emotional referent intended. Shattering any sense of plot and sustaining no literal interpretation, his approach to movement sequencing relies largely on chance operations. The dance derives its rhythm not from a music preconceived and imposed from without, but from the very nature of the step or of the phrases, and from the dancer's own musculature. A movement is thus expressive of nothing else but itself. Yet, if the interest of such a dance resides in its own consummate physicality rather than in its ability to reveal what is verbally inaccessible, it is precisely because dance here refuses to encode the "natural." It "denaturalizes" the body by disengaging itself from the quest for a so-called organic choreographic process, which often dwells on a narrow concept of the discursive, hence remaining blind as to how subject and body come into being and how every dance participates in a given discourse.

By acknowledging no "natural" ties between movement and feelings, or between feeling and meaning, Cunningham's dances invalidate the tradition of cultivating binary oppositions between mind and heart, thought and action. Such tradition tends in this case to sanctify intuitive feelings in its endless attempts to berate or exclude verbal expression. (This, precisely in a society marked with the stamp of dualistic rationalism, where demonstrative reasoning and explanatory discourse dominate, and where in the name of *logos*, all forms of the "non-verbal" are dismissed and defined negatively as non-sense, non-reason, non-truth, or non-reality.) When dance is no more and no less than "a moving image of life," the performance of movement in space is also much less a display of the spectacular, virtuoso perfected body, than it is a full and evenly passionate execution of pedestrian activities, in which the articulate body can be said to be at best, *musically accurate*. In Cunningham's words, "through this devotion to mindful movement the dancer achieves technical competence that manifests itself in flexible responses to novel situations."[10]

A Moment In and Out of Time

The traditional aesthetic ideals that pervaded all of the Japanese arts and accomplishments have been summarized largely in the concept of *yugen*. A performance may be said to possess *yugen*—the mark of supreme attainment—when, for example, a gesture, which is beautiful in itself, is also a gateway to something else. *Yugen*, translated as the Unfathomable, is often used to suggest the profound and remote as well as the tranquil and elegant: the aspects of things that cannot easily be translated into words, and often lead to a blind alley as far as verbalism is concerned. Attempts to find equivalences to *yugen* in Western literatures have, for example, resorted to Edgar Poe's "suggestive indefiniteness of vague and therefore of spiritual effect;" or else, to T. S. Eliot's "moment in and out of time."[11]

Noh spectators, as related by Zeami, sometimes delighted in the moments of "no-action," which they considered to be the most enjoyable ones of the performance. Occurring in between two actions, these are the moments when both the music and the actor's movements come to a stop. Yet, instead of slackening while the dancing, the singing, the dialogues, or the different types of miming are suspended, the actor maintains an "unwavering inner strength," manifesting thereby the spirit of his role more intensely than through all his other modes of performance. Much of the pleasure of the spectators is due here to this underlying spiritual strength, whose presence should also remain an absence, as it cannot visibly be shown. For, "if it is obvious," Zeami specified, "it becomes an act, and is no longer 'no-action'."[12]

Moments of suspension not only expand the imagination and stimulate interest, they also move the audience in ways that no music, dancing or role-playing can. The performance is determined both by the actions performed and by the in-betweens of

these actions. Far from being merely "a man of action," as Grotowski defines him, the Performer is here also a person of no-action. Or, at least, the kind of (spiritual) "action" involved in such moments of (physical) no-action defies the limits of the visible and the audible. It exceeds the arts of the skin and the flesh. Noted philosopher Nishida Kitaro (1870–1945) almost seemed to echo the opinion of Zeami's Noh spectators when he made the following comparison: "In contradistinction to Western culture which considers form as existence and formation as good, the urge to see the form of the formless, and hear the sound of the soundless lies at the foundation of Eastern culture."[13]

Although the difference between East and West can hardly be so conclusive, still, in traditional Japanese and Chinese aesthetics, one is often made aware that the form expressed is never really intended to express form, but rather, the Formless. As with the *haiku* which draws its poetic effect from the effortlessness and infiniteness of its "surplus meaning," a painting with *yugen*—also translated in this context as Subtle Profundity or Deep Reserve—enables us "to feel infinite reverberations" without having to resort to minute detailing.[14] A similar comparison can be made between the white unpainted area, which constitutes the very soul of such a painting, and the visibly-formless-audibly-soundless moment of Noh theater, which Zeami designated as "the undone interval" (*senuhima*) of pause. Wrote the master:

> Often critical acclaim rests on the idea that "parts left undone stimulate interest." This is a secret point of assurance for the performer. Say that there are two measures of music for which he must assume the proper stances and all the various body postures. The parts left undone, then, refer to the interval of pause . . . [But] it is no good for this sense of inward awareness to visibly show, for were it to show anywhere it would become a mannerism and so cease to be "undone." In this artless balance, in this peace of mind when one's thoughts are lost even to oneself, the undone interval links that which came before and that which is to follow. This in itself is the sensitivity which unites the whole of art.[15]

An Artless Balance

While being beautiful in itself, a gesture with *yugen*, as mentioned earlier, is also "a gateway to something else." The performer never loses sight of the "correct balance" (Zeami) between spiritual and physical actions, or between the painted and unpainted surfaces of a performance. (With the understanding that "correct" here does not refer to an order imposed from the outside or to a preconceived set of values, but to a precision that arises from the [non-] gesture in itself—a "musically accurate" [non-] gesture.) Furthermore, Subtle Profundity inscribes a form of darkness, one that calms and stills the mind, clearing the way for renewed creativity. As a musician from India puts it, "repose is . . . the secret of getting in tune with that aspect of life which is the essence of all things."[16] Since action and stillness mutually define each other; since a painting is determined as much by its filled-in surfaces as by those left undone; since a body can only structure space while being structured by it, a performance that includes no interval of pause is no doubt also one that "needs tuning."

Tambura players, for example, are said to tune their own soul while they tune their instrument. Such tuning constitutes a performance of its own, and the listeners, likewise, need to tune themselves to the music while appreciating the way the musicians sing into a chord. As the latter become concentrate, they also tune themselves to their audience. They usually have no program beforehand and do not know what they will perform next. Yet each time, they are inspired to sing a certain song or to play in a certain mode.[17] Tuning outwardly, tuning inwardly: these are other intervals of pause, which, to many music lovers, often prove to be more enjoyable than the real piece of music itself. In the process of tuning, a subject becomes a poem effortlessly; what is brought about in time is not the search for a given pitch—the standard A or the preconceived correct chord which constitutes the universalized measure of perfection in Western musical traditions. On the contrary, what progressively materializes is an "artless balance" through which takes shape, each time differently, the evolving pitch to be shared among performers, listeners and instruments played. After all, to recall a statement by Peter Sellars, in the ongoing process of becoming isn't every single performance a rehearsal?[18]

"Men must learn to be silent," novelist and film director Marguerite Duras affirms. "They are the ones who started to speak, to speak alone and for everyone else . . . They immediately forced women and extremists to keep silent. They activated the old language, enlisted the aid of the old way of theorizing, in order to relate, to recount, to explain this new situation . . ."[19] The encounter with silence—the moment in and out of time, not quite unreal nor quite real—is precisely what allows a text to vibrate and to breathe. In women's contexts, the reality of silence is further complicated by the fact that the coming into and breaking away from language is at once a necessity, a discovery, and a damnation. For language, as is well known, is a site of both empowerment and enslavement. Women's literature, in Duras' words, is often "translated from darkness. Women have been in darkness for centuries. They don't know themselves. Or only poorly." So to translate, she may have to "make darkness the point of departure in judging what men call light." She may have to tip the balance in order to find her balance. And she may find herself facing a vast "undone interval of pause"—a world of suspension—in which, more than ever, occupied territories saturate the field of vision. "When I write," confides Duras, "there is something that becomes silent. I let something take over inside me . . . It's as if I were returning to a wild country. Nothing is concerted. Perhaps before everything else, before being Duras, I am—simply—a woman . . ."[20]

Making Music with Painting

A wild country. Where writing constantly solicits the interval of silence. Where, even when speech is no longer, words continue to move, borne on the echoes of women's voices. Duras tuning herself to the unknown ends up meeting with her simplest self: being a woman. The gap left unoccupied becomes a silent multivalent transitional space, whose fragrance and reverberations can only make themselves felt through an artless balancing of abstinence from display/speech and the urge to create/speak everything anew. In Duras' films, Pierre Félida wrote, for example, that her writing "gives birth to a strange speech; speech which moves in that inner zone of silence where the power of hearing is *spoken* and where voices can intrude upon the echoes of fragmented words . . . This speech is terrifying because no narrative can contain it nor prevent its shiftings nor even guarantee a boundary to what is opened up by it and in it."[21]

Of great importance but rarely developed to its limits in cinema is the compass of the voice and the way its presence and absence musically structure the filmic space. Working with voices and working with actors are not necessarily the same. Voices and actors move in spaces that at times meet synchronously or interact in syncopation, and other times have nothing to do with one another, except through a process of transformation, in which effects of rupture are likely to challenge the way the media's economy of suture produces an entire class of inattentive viewers/makers who see without seeing and hear without hearing. What are questioned in such a practice are not only the homogeneity between voice and image, but also the compartmentalization of sensual and/or intellectual faculties. Voice is breath. A wo/man's breath manifested outwardly, the sound and color of a voice are, in fact, one and the same: movement. *Color is heard* when sound is most visible and least audible; and reciprocally, *sound is seen* when color is most audible and least visible. In the rupturing of realistic effect of the filmic image, the relationship between voice, sound and silence transforms itself and becomes musicalized.

Music lies both at the source of creation and in the means of absorbing it. "There is terror in noise," drummer Mickey Hart intently remarks, "and in that terror there is also power."[22] The name is the same for that *other* power or de-power—of freeing noise and rhythm. Light and life. Everywhere one looks, one sees rhythm. Every physical illness, indeed, is a musical dis-ease. Change is inscribed in noise, and as a reflection of power, the control of noise remains fundamentally political. In a musicalized relationship where everything possesses a rhythmic value, an image or a sound always has the potential to be *other* than what it is. Thus, although cinema remains a highly guarded territory, Duras (whose films, because of the risks they take, often give the viewer the feeling of assisting to the birth of cinema) can still affirm: "It's because my cinema scarcely exists as cinema that I can make these films. The type of perfection to which mainstream cinema aspires (in its use of clever technique with the sole aim of maintaining order) is accurately inscribed in its precise adherence to prevailing social codes . . . Mainstream cinema can be very clever, but it is rarely intelligent."[23]

To show everything, to gloss over the operation of suture, and to catch a reality "as it is," is to condemn it to the *cliché* and to leave nothing to the imagination. Asserts Dionys Mascolo: "The cinema was born stupid because it was born powerful . . . It is stupid like Power."[24] So unless an image unsettles itself from its naturalized state, it acquires no resonance and is bound to remain flat—that is, unmusical hence lifeless. Creating does not merely consist of deforming or inventing a character within a situation, but rather of drawing new relationships between people and things as they exist. Everything is in the differing, displacing and rearticulating of intervals. Yet, as Zeami acutely warned, intervals cannot be forged. To maintain the vitality of an image-sound-silence that reverberates, stimulates as well as empties out the eye/I, for example, radically means to put oneself in an intense state of non-knowingness and of curiosity, living thereby fully the contemporaneity of bodies and movements, while also being able to exceed the moment in the present. Filmmaking thus thrives on the desire to see with and beyond the fragment; to envision what is left out or remains necessarily undone; hence, to sustain infinite surprises in a finite frame.

"The real antonym of the 'poetic' is not the prosaic, but the stereotyped," wrote Roland Barthes.[25] Zeami, Chiyo, Basho, Grotowski, Cunningham, the Tambura players, Duras, and the list goes on. The poetic leap can hardly be achieved through self-explanatory links between names and practices. To solicit new relationships, a space is opened up, which will have to remain unoccupied despite the many engagements between the dissimilar itineraries that crisscross it. Nothing, indeed, stands more acutely in opposition to the poetic than the stereotype, which is not necessarily a false, but rather an arrested representation of a shifting reality. The constant challenge faced in dealing with stereotypes is precisely that of assuming representation without being limited to it (to *return* freely to representation, the potential of a form to *depart* from representation must be affirmed and set into motion). The challenge is also that of placing the viewers in relation to the subject filmed—not as one routinely places them according to some visual and aural habits (the *clichés*), but as one places oneself blindly according to one's own unpredictable impressions and feelings. To quote filmmaker Robert Bresson, "The beauty of your film will not lie in the images (postcardism), but in the *ineffable* that they will emanate."[26]

The story goes that when Basho asked his teacher and pupil, samurai Kyoroku, why he liked painting, the latter said it was because of poetry. "And why do you love poetry?" Basho continued. "Because of painting," Kyoroku replied. It seems appropriate here to borrow Basho's happy conclusion and to say that, since Confucian tradition has decreed it is shameful for a person to have many accomplishments, it is only adequate that s/he should excel in making one use of several arts.[27] But what can "excel" mean when placed in this context of "slender margin between the real and the unreal" (Monzaemon)? Perhaps an example can also be found here in the well-known case of Jean-Luc Godard—one of the filmmakers who consistently refuses to abide by the Western tradition of setting, in the name of Pure Vision or of Communication, a mutually exclusive relation between writing and painting or between the verbal and the visual. For this much fetishized giant of cinema (of the Left), the "incredible" is what people don't see, and indeed, the camera constitutes "only a moment"—at times more, and at other times less powerful than other (off-camera) moments.

Much has been said on how Godard's film work defies the finished product to offer a process that unfolds in front of the viewers—above all, as an activity of production. His scripts, always written as the filming and rehearsal evolve, incorporate simultaneously the actions on and off camera, in and out of the performing self. His highly controversial interchange with actors is both condemned and praised for being "execrable" and "baffling," since the roles they are supposed to play never exist prior to their performances, and the actors never quite know what they are fabricating at the moment of fabrication. What can be said of the reception of Cunningham's dances does apply very well here to Godard's films. In the multiply diverse references to the world that interactions between performers offer to the audience, the experience of each viewer like that of each performer is unique, not merely because individuals differ in their background and actualities, but also because each of them has literally seen/heard/felt/made a different dance/film. As the participants' moves are mutually defined by one another, each response is a performance of its own. Reflecting on women's representation in Godard's films, Julia Kristeva thus concluded: "His modest pretension is not to propose solutions, but to show, through hints, without really unveiling. Rarely has the image come so close to the ellipsis."[28]

Godard's "wild gestuality" in the filmic space (projected, for example, in the way a violinist fences the visual space with his bow; the way people and cars suddenly enter the frame; the way they move restlessly in all directions or collide violently with one another) excels in making use of more than one art to open the boundaries of what constitutes cinema. It has earned him many labels, including that of a "Beethoven composing a film with two violins, a viola and a violoncello," or that of a painter whose combinations of color in painting are "so accurate, yet so unreasonable." An anecdote related by painter Bernard Dufour further exposes how Godard reflexively proceeds with his "paintings." Invited to visit and draw in Godard's studio in Geneva when the latter started work on *Passion*, Dufour came with his working tools. Scarcely had he started drawing in the manner of Poussin that Godard, shooting with his video camera, asked him to draw with his eyes closed. Dufour agreed to the challenge and started a new drawing of the soldier in *Massacre des Innocents*. As expected, Dufour momentarily got lost as he lifted his right hand, which held the pen. However, he succeeded—bumpily—to complete the drawing by finding again with his left hand the memory, the muscular trace of the necessary position of the right hand. Dufour was then led to conclude that this "perverse childishness" and delirious project of making a painter draw with eyes closed, denying thereby his very essence, not only became a terrific investigation of Godard's own work; it also "set into relief the eternal hours of acquisition of 'knowledge by rote' only to end in the discovery of a 'I don't know' if not a 'I can't'."[29]

A new way of writing, hence of feeling. The anecdote further suggests that to "excel" in "returning to a wild country" is to realize this artless balance in performance, to live and let live these undone intervals of pause where knowledge acquired remains suspended in non-knowingness (Basho's change and permanence). Where inter-arts/inter-cultures involve, not the accumulation or the melting of previously identified objects, competences and frontiers, but the discovery of different objects produced by new multiple competences in different situations across different cultures. Something is being born that invalidates the institutional/professional division between "painting" and "writing," East and West. This newly formed formless sensitivity bears, in fact, the trace of an old name: curiosity. A name that materializes itself anew each time, inscribing accordingly the variety of context and the specificity of circumstance. Wrote Bresson: "I dream about my film gradually forming itself under the look, like a painter's eternally fresh canvas;"[30] and Godard: "Cinema is the art of making music with painting."[31]

III

no end in sight

Mother's Talk

First published in *The Politics of M(Othering): Womanhood, Identity and Resistance in African Literature,* ed. Obioma Nnaemeka (London: Routledge, 1997), pp. 26–32.

> When memory goes a-gathering firewood, it
> brings back the sticks that strike its fancy
> —Birago Diop

"The most stupid of all animals that fly, walk and swim, that live beneath the ground, in water, or in the air, are undoubtedly crocodiles, which crawl on land and walk at the bottom of the water . . . And this, for no other reason than that they have the best memories in the world." This is how Senegalese poet and storyteller Birago Diop begins the tale of Mother Crocodile.[1] This is how he recounts a narrative of his elders, which he ascribes to another teller—the *griot* (storyteller, singer, and genealogist) Amadou Koumba. And, to complicate matters further, this is also what Amadou Koumba said he remembered from another teller yet, for "that is not my opinion, said Amadou Koumba. That is what Golo the monkey says. And although everyone agrees that Golo is the most coarsely spoken of all the creatures, since he is their *griot,* he sometimes manages to make the most sensible remarks, so some say; or at least to make us believe he has made them, according to others."

Stupidity and Memory

Talking brought three male-identified voices together while deferring their unity. The story presents itself as a piece of gossip that circulates from teller to teller. The man who narrates (Diop) implicitly warns the reader that he is quoting Amadou Koumba who actually got it from Golo-the-He-Monkey. Right at the outset, the question is raised as to the real source of such a gossip: if the reader can't really tell whether Golo makes "sensible remarks" or whether he simply takes the lead in making people believe that he is the one to have made them, then whose opinion is it exactly? As the tale progresses, storytelling becomes increasingly reflexive and the reader is further led to ask, who among the tellers is the real monkey? Whose stupidity is it finally? Here lies the power of indirection in which the tale weavers excel. Through the spell of words the latter must both resonate the comments passed on and fulfill the function of the tale, which is not merely to deliver a message, but rather to invite talk around it.

The postponed subject of the tale, the loved–hated figure that elicits mockery from the male tellers but is talked about only with much caution, is here the most persevering storyteller of all: Mother Crocodile Diassigue. A tale's resonance lies in its ability to proceed by indirection and by sharp digressions. Nobody understood this better than Diassigue who educated her children with his/stories of men—"not of Crocodiles, for crocodiles have no his/stories." Mother always remembers. And what she remembers, she never forgets to weave it with what her mother, her grandmother, her great grandmother remembered. Diassigue, the mother of crocodiles, was thus reputed for her very good memory. "And much as he deplored this, in his heart of hearts Golo had to admit it," wrote Diop. As for her being stupid, "it was difficult to tell whether Golo's statement was intended to be praise or blame." The saddest part of the whole business, however, was that Diassigue's own children, the little crocodiles, began to share the monkeys' opinion of their mother and to think that Golo spoke the truth. "They thought that perhaps their mother really did sometimes talk a lot of nonsense." So goes the tale, which proceeds to tell us how Diassigue, the all-absorbing spectator, remembered best because she spent her time, from her lair in the mud or under the sunny banks of the river, watching the movements of life, lending a patient ear to the chatter of women and of other living creatures, and thus collecting all the news and noises of her talkative environment.

Wisdom and Memory

—Here is a story!
—A story it is.
—It has happened.
—It has already been told.

When Mother gathered her children around her and told them what she and her foremothers had seen, they yawned and yawned. For while they dreamt of great crocodile exploits, all they could hear were stories of black men and white men. Having witnessed "empires born and kingdoms die," the mothers were only eager to recount the times when the river turned red with corpses after the coming and going of men. And what they remembered of places, events, and passers-by was, in fact, no more and no less relevant to the crocodiles than the history of men, of wars, of massacres of men by other men. One day, it was said, alerted three times by the disturbing messages of the crows, Diassigue hurriedly collected her children to urge them to leave their home, for "the Emir of Tzara has declared war on the Wolofs." To her youngest son's question, "What difference does it make to us crocodiles if the Wolofs of Wolo fight against the Moors of Tzara?" she then replied, "My child, the dry grass can set fire to the green grass. Let us go." But the little ones would not follow their mother. To shorten Diop's tale, at the end of seven days of terrible fighting, the Moors lost and the Wolofs won, taking with them the heir to the Moorish kingdom who bore a wound in his right side.

All the priests and medicine men were summoned to care for the young captive prince, but to no avail. Finally, there came to the court an old, old woman who prescribed the effective remedy, which was: "to apply, three times a day, to the sore place, the fresh brain of a young crocodile."

"The tale is of all countries," wrote literary critic Mohamadou Kane.[2] Referred to as "the loyal mirror of African sensibility and wisdom," it is, of all literary genres, the one to circulate the most, and its extreme mobility has led literary critics to proclaim it not only the best genre to depict rural life, but also one whose continuity and variety cuts across cultural and ethnic boundaries. While remaining specific to local events, customs and landscapes, the tale also functions as a depersonalizing, hence a generalizing tool for initiating talk around a moral instruction. Each society has its own treasure house from which its culture draws in order to live, and it is precisely through storytelling that one is said to encounter the genius of a people. To (re) tell stories is "to enter into the constant recreation of the world, of community, of mankind."[3] Talking therefore brings the impossible within reach. It contributes to widening the horizon of one's imagination; to constantly shifting the frontier between reality and fantasy; and to questioning, through the gifts of the so-called supernatural and the unusual, the limits of all that is thought to be "ordinary" and "believable."

Wisdom's Gender

Nothing seems more ordinary in the tale of Mother Crocodile than the gendered construction of wisdom. Diassigue is here presented both as a palaverer and a wise matron. Typically, Mother's talk is exasperating, nonsensical, at the same time as it is perilously clairvoyant and caringly farsighted. By persisting in remembering, it tends to overplay and to reiterate the immorality of men's his/stories. The division set up between the worlds of crocodiles and of men is one that differentiates not only animals from humans, but also mothertellers from fathertellers, warfleers from warmakers, sapience from stupidity. African folklore abounds with stories and proverbs whose moral is to caution men against women's supposedly most treacherous shortcoming: their indiscretion. "Give your love to the woman, but do not trust her"[4] remains, for example, one of the best advices a man can give another man. Utterly incapable of holding their tongues when they are asked to keep a secret (in a male-is-norm world), women are repeatedly depicted as those who "work their tongues so much harder than their hands," and they are always seen chattering away nineteen to the dozen.

Wisdom is here at the heart of the struggle of memory against forgetting. Without it, history is bound to repeat itself blindly; and access to the forces of the surreal is impossible, for the surreal universe is hidden from men by the screen of the real. To be able to see beyond sensible manifestations is to understand that "A thing is always itself and more than itself."[5] Mother's prosy knowledge of men's his/stories is, in fact, no ordinary gossip. In the village environment, idle talk may contribute to the communal mapping of the social terrain, while ill-considered talk is likely to sow dissension in the group. As the result of the compilation work of several generations of mothers, Diassigue's history-informed accounts could neither be reduced to trivial interpersonal reactions among women, nor can they be attributed to any malevolently divisive intent. On the

contrary, if these accounts recalled the deeds of the great men of Black Africa, it was mainly to display the continuity of violence and of wars in men's world; wars which had already forced her grandmother to leave her home, the Senegal River, only to encounter everywhere else, in her search for peaceful waters, more killings and more corpses.

Commonly enough, however, Mother's dignified speeches failed to command (men's) respect. (It is, indeed, significant that the child who questioned Diassigue's decision to leave home at the break of war, was her *youngest son*.) What was believable from mothers to daughters may become (temporarily) unbelievable in the process of transmitting men's his/stories (to crocodiles). "A woman will find ninety-nine lies, but she will betray herself with the hundredth," says a Hausa proverb;[6] while a multitude of Fulani sayings warn: "If your mother has prepared food, eat; if she has concocted [a plan for you], refuse;" because "He who follows a woman's plan, is bound to drown." Or else: "One does not confide in a woman," for "A woman is the fresh water that kills, the shallow water that drowns."[7] In many African folktales, male wisdom thus departs markedly from female wisdom. The wisdom attributed to men is one that generally works at conserving the social group, while the wisdom attributed to women is consistently equated with a supernatural malefic power. She who appears in almost every tale in the form of "an old, old woman" often holds powers that are both maleficent and beneficent, black-and-white magic. She can operate wonders, she can heal and make dreams come true at will; but she can also kill, punish and prompt irrevocable losses. As she names death, Death appears.

Talk, More (Than) Talk

> —A story is coming!
> —A story.
> —Let it go, let it come.
> . . .
> —Call it back!
> —It has already started. It cannot be called back.

Destructive wisdom remains the prerogative of women. Such a clear (unacknowledged) moral implication is likely to be divisive, but even in its divisiveness it should remain open to talk, if the function of storytelling in African contexts is to be respected. The moral retrieved from the tale of Mother Crocodile can easily be: "Always listen to the wisdom of the elders." But a gendered reading of this same tale can hardly be content with such a genderless generalization. The reader remembers, instead, that it was through a deferred male voice that we were told the story of a female character who failed to spellbind her children with tales of wondrous men (she equally failed to indulge in tales of crocodile exploits). And as the story drew to its "last word," the reader is again abruptly faced with another female character—albeit "an old, old woman"—who succeeded in healing the young captive prince by dooming the destiny of the young crocodiles. Once the healing words of malediction are let out, they cannot be taken back. Thus, She warns first, then She acts accordingly: for whoever remembers her words with good intent, She cures; while for those who neglect, forget, or use them with ill intent, her punishment is irrepealable. If the crocodiles had disobeyed their mother, it was largely due to the fact that they trusted the immediate *believability* of Golo-the-He-Monkey's words and their vision stopped at the *screen of the real* (the illusory separation of the animals' world from that of the humans). They had, in other words, sided with the men (whether the latter praise or blame) in judging mother, and had thus failed to recognize that mother's talk was talk but also more than talk.

> Ho! Call the women
> call the women
> I didn't know what it means
> to be a woman
> if I knew
> I would have changed into a bird
> in the bush
> if I could not changed into a bird
> in the bush
> I would have changed into a hind
> in the bush
> to be married
> is a misfortune
> not to be married
> is a misfortune
> I would have changed into a bird
> in the bush
> to have a child
> is a misfortune
> not to have a child
> is a misfortune
> I would have changed into a hind
> in the bush
> call the women
> call the women
> I didn't know what it means
> to be a woman

(A song by women in Mali)[8]

Talk is what it takes to expose motherhood in all its ambivalences. Mothering is exalted only so long as women either conscientiously conform to their role as guardians of the status quo and protectors of the established order, or they perform a fairy godmother's task of fulfilling harmless wishes, dreams and desire. Since wisdom may be defined as a form of knowledge based on *discretion*, it is not readily perceived as knowledge by the unwise, and cannot be measured or controlled in a system of power relations dependent on accumulative, factual knowledge. The need to contain and restrict women's wisdom within the mothering role is therefore a constant in social institutions across cultures; and women's status as child bearer continues in many African contexts to be the test of their womanhood. From one generation to another, mothers are called upon to perfect their duty as the killjoy keepers of tradition—especially in matters that concern their gender. As is well known, a woman's lot is to conceive, bear, feed and above all, indoctrinate her children. The tale of Mother Crocodile revolves, typically enough, round Diassigue's role as educator. In the process of transmitting knowledge, women are held solely responsible for their children's errors. No matter how unfailing Diassigue's memory was when it recounted the historical deeds of great men, because she failed to convince her own offspring of the value of Mother's words, the entire crocodile species would have to suffer the die-hard reputation of being . . . brainless.

Tale Telling and the Texture of Memory

Mother's knowledge is always discreet in its indiscretion. She may fail in speech (as women often do when speaking means inserting themselves into the patriarchal socio-symbolic order), and she may be so "indiscreet" as to compel her male companions to arm themselves with a thousand strategies to defend the "men's secrets." (Unless a man wishes to bring about his own downfall, affirms a Senegalese man, he should not confide in women for "they don't know what is essential.") But her word is paradoxically kept as the word of truth—of what has been, what is, and what will be. Says a Fulani proverb, "The speech [that stays] in the belly is the child of your mother, the speech [that springs] from your mouth is the child of your father."[9] What marks Mother's talk, therefore, is a practice of indirection that is at times overt and other times secret. Like a historian, Diassigue filled her stories with factual names, places and events, and the indirect took shelter under the figures of the direct and of verifiable accounts about great men. But when the time came to warn her children of the imminent danger of men's war, Mother's wisdom preferred the secret of truth in this overtly indirect reply: "My child, the dry grass can set fire to the green grass."

In the politics of remembering, public opinion maintains a reduced conception of memory. It is apparently always opposed to obliviousness and identified with the power to recall what has been learned. Thus, says the tale, the neglect of memory leads to the loss of brain—hence the notoriously unequaled stupidity of those who dare to defy memory, the family of crocodile. Reverse this logic à la monkey, and the talk will continue. If crocodiles are stupid for no other reason than that they have the best memories, then whoever remembers the story of crocodiles' memories and carries it on must be . . . abysmally stupid. These are, for example, the storytellers and story commentators who praise and blame, who talk to initiate talk, who write to invite writing, and who can only laugh at mother-memory by laughing at themselves and their function—as repositories of creative tradition and as transmitters of the genius of a people. Once set in motion, the story that strikes their fancy is both irreversible and infinitely shifting. An assertion of gentleness, Mother's talk does not let itself

be caught, for kindness belongs to no system; it stands at the limit of the tale's moral. As she speaks, she crosses limits, she remembers the texture of memory and if she loses, she loses without losing. The loss of brain, for some, is the healing of an open wound, for others. After all, it is said with much insight that "Poetry has to be a bit stupid" (Pushkin).[10]

So my story ends

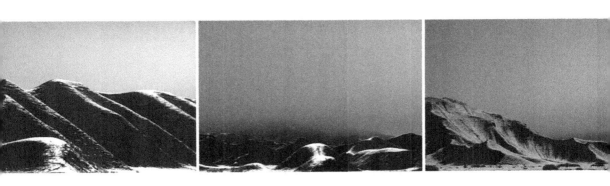

The Desert is Watching (2003) and *L'Autre marche* (2006–2009)

White Spring

First published in *The Dream of the Audience: Theresa Hak Kyung Cha (1951–1982)*, ed. C. M. Lewallen (Berkeley: University of California Press, 2001), pp. 33–50.

It's a dream, one says waking up in silence, and now? One wonders whether one has just dreamt a silence or whether silence is the sound of a dream. The entire room brims with incandescent silence. One sees not a thing with one's eyes open and one perks one's ears up: no, not even the faint echo of an I. And yet, somewhere nearby, something is silently beaming in recognition. White moon, dark earth, light writing. Try to frame that beam into visibility, and it will quickly fade out from view. Try to touch it, even with the darker hand, and soon the lighter hand yearning for proof will reach out in earnest, depriving it of its freedom to disappear. Protective and well meaning, perhaps the hand merely forgets to draw back *in time* for the radiance to flare up on its own. In the passage from light to light container or from dream to dream reading, always lurking is the risk of emptying out the very space of dream and, further, of preventing dreamlands from rising out of sleeping bodies.

Here, where the black moon shines; there, where the white pathway fades into the night; between reverie and resistance lies a familiar face: that of the Absent—the artist-poet who assumes the ancient role both of a medium and of a magnetizer. To her falls the magical task of resurrecting voices and looks by letting shadows appear and speak in her folds. The maker-recipient is bound to dream in one and in multiplicity: *no end in sight*. Today, like every day, as I return to a room sealed with darkness, a vibration immediately starts flickering, while a light window etches itself onto my mind. On the white surface of the virtual screen, an image as she partly described it appears: in a dim performance space, separated from the viewer by a cheesecloth curtain whose effect is that of "an opaque transparency," the performer slowly moves about in a candle-lit, oval-shaped area, wearing a white robe and unfurling twenty meters of black and red cloth from underneath. As they are set loose in the performer's choreographed gestures, she becomes entwined in them. Movement and stillness, sound and silence are carefully highlighted, for her wish in this piece as she wrote it, is "to be the dream of the audience" (*A Ble Wail*, performance 1975).[1]

She makes her appearance here as Theresa Hak Kyung Cha, and she is many. (Yet within sight, few are those of us for whom black has no opposite: neither set up against anything nor equated with nothing.) Many, I remember from the time when I first encountered her work. I had then returned to the States from a long stay in Senegal and was embarking on a writing journey with *Woman, Native, Other* after having just completed the film *Reassemblage*. 1982: the year says it all; it marked a full turning point for Cha, as for me. I recognized the tone, the cuts, the wait, the twilight—halfway between night unearthing and day re-veiling. The two lights (not one, not two either), on which reason and analysis have nothing to say. I recognized the voice—plural and utterly singular. A blind voice walking bare-foot into the heart of (our) shadows. Through it, I heard, within a closer range of resonance, the voices of WoMen: mother and the foremothers of Korea (Yu Guan Soon, Ahn Joong Kun and the historical voices of resistance); some of Cha's past "elsewhere" (including Sappho, the nine muses of Greek mythology, Sister Thérèse, Joan of Arc); and some of our shared cultural whereabouts, including Marguerite Duras (her mirror-voices hunted down by death in love), Samuel Beckett (his mis-said, mis-seen, three-moment-in-one Other), or else, Stéphane Mallarmé (his Shadow and his muse[s]—*La morte qui parle*, the dead woman who speaks). My fall into Cha's work was at once a chance encounter and an inevitable one. When two strangers meet and become friends, lovers or companions, it is often said in Asia that "their paths are bound to cross" and that they are merely resolving a past debt. This is so, not necessarily because we share a similar background or interests as commonly thought, but perhaps because without planning it, we find ourselves entering the same spring.

> You remain dismembered with the belief that magnolia blooms white even on seemingly dead branches and you wait.
>
> (Dictée, 1982, p. 155)[2]

The Page Screen

The inky way has its own law—to create and to break. Leaving, it returns— *Aller/Retour*—slowly imploding with the sign, with its share of meaning and of death. Between verb and noun, daydreams, night dreams come and go, feeding upon one another until no reality can be proven real, and no dream is only a dream. Now that I've seen it also white on black, I can hardly find the words for it. And yet, there's no other way to go forward but to return to black on white—maintained but by the word's own dreamtime. Language speaks of she who speaks. Syllables, words, fragments of sentences return, linger and occupy vast territories of the mind, even and especially when they are uninvited. Sometimes they move away, slide, slip, stick and sting, creating odd lapses. They disappear when solicited and without warning re-appear. Silence them and they may go on speaking volumes while absent, coerce them into prefabricated lines and they may yield through their stilted presence nothing more and nothing less than a form of silence.

Strange is the way language and memory operate, but stranger still is the pervasive need of ours to track the words for fear of going off the rails of access and communication. In trying to relate the dream and to write it down, we tend to focus on the storyline, thereby threatening the dream to disappear quickly into illegibility. Accounts and analyses (of a work or of someone's life hi-story) built on storylines heavily (if not exclusively) based on chronology and on external retrievable facts (the one privileged path to the gate of Approval) prove to be limiting and at times, despairingly inadequate.

> It's as if writing were something outside you, in a tangle of senses: between writing and having written, having written and having to go on writing; between knowing and not knowing what it's all about; starting from complete meaning, being submerged by it, and ending up in meaninglessness. The image of a black block in the middle of the world isn't far out.
>
> (Marguerite Duras)[3]

Comment taire? The question raised is not simply how to keep the silence, to stay quiet or to hold one's tongue, but how not to say while saying. In French and English, on black-and-white pages, with black-and-white letters, Cha's *Commentaire*[4] (text and photo, 1981) offers in its spatial and linear layout of the words, the possibility of a comment or a commentary that includes a *comment taire*—that is, a *comment*/how to and a *taire*/silence, be silent. And further, depending on how one reads sequences, one may through meaning or through music draw indefinite links between "*comme*/ as like/ tear/ moment/ arily/ two hold/ tongue hold/ to one more/ and more/ time/ takes/ to hush." As with Cha's other works, reading is intimacy shared in night labor. Engaging language as simultaneously seen and heard, her writing plays up the arbitrary relation between the sound of a word, its visual spelling, its multiple referents and its foreign mate in translation.

By the alternating dark and bright layout of *Commentaire* one is invited to scan the words while quickly leafing through the pages. One follows, as with film, the effect of a variable flickering of light and the illusion of a movement generated within the given space. Through these black-and-white surfaces, *écran sur écran*, screen on screen, one catches sight of *blancheur* (whiteness) and *noirceur* (blackness) punctuated in their comings and goings by *blanchir* (whiten), *blanchiment*, *blanchissement* (whitening). And, by the motion into white or black, into the page emptied of letters. Particularly striking is the dreamy effect of the photograph of a film screen gone white in a movie theater where, apparently unaffected by its hazy glare, singles and couples are seen giving way to sleep here and there with empty seats all around. The work ends the way it begins—with a film still and with black—moving from bordered to non-bordered pages that close in on all white then on all black, until the white comes to the fore and what is left is the empty page framed by black: the papery version of a film screen.

> The white mist rising everywhere, constant gathering and dispersing. This is how it fills the screen . . .
>> Lift me up to the window the white frame and the glass between, early dusk or dawn when light is muted, lines yield to shades, houses cast shadow pools in the passing light. Brief. All briefly towards night.
>
> (Dictée, pp. 112; 179)

Comment? How? Answers, if answers are what one wants, can be found anytime everywhere one cares to look. Although they may come one by one to one's limited ear, they show up and take leave by the thousands when the whole of a body listens to life and death. Answers, if answers there are to this impossible "how," are written, translated and realized all over Cha's work. One would have to enter the dream—even if one only has a shred of it to dwell in—and wait until it gives off words, like fragrances from burnt incense. Following Cha in her "twenty meters of black and red cloth from underneath," I first come across the wound and the needle of Astronomy:

> It takes her seconds less to break the needle off its body in attempt to collect the loss directly from the wound. Stain begins to absorb the material spilled on . . . Something of the ink that resembles the stain from the interior emptied onto emptied into emptied upon this boundary this surface . . . Expel. Ne te cache pas. Révèle toi. Sang. Encre. Of its body's extention of its containment.
>
> (Dictée, p. 65)

Repeating for a bit of memory, I would have to wait until the stain from the interior absorbs the material (not the other way around as commonly said), until the blood (*sang*) or the ink (*encre*) reveals itself, emptied upon the surface. Red inside when alive, it turns inky as it leaves its imprint, so that "Year and year it rained. The stone pavement stained where you [my brother] fell still remains dark" (Dictée, p. 85). The rain, the stone, the speech, the memory of a dream that was no dream. A dream called "History, the old wound."

Unwinding, she *tears* open the wound while healing from underneath out. *Taire. How to tear. Two hold.* Red thread, black thread, the course inside the line outside, both in one, from body to page, screen upon screen, fluids are spilled, shadows take on the allure of reality. Here, the tie that binds along the bloodline: family, ethnicity, nation. There, the string of language and writing that defines her very activities—as a writer and a visual and performance artist. Each thread pulled up turns out to be a multiplicity of threads, all receded from view under the white robe and seen only through the cheesecloth curtain. Holding on to the threads, now displaced in space and in time, I am inevitably led back here to "the white frame and *the glass between*" (my italics). Blood, ink, rain. In the transformative process, substance becomes surface. Images of these two and one waters by which traces vanish to return "stain glass glassy" repeatedly arise in her voice-image repertoire, and again and again, in numerously shifting signs, one is reminded that separating the spectator and the performer is: "an opaque transparency."

The blinds, the gauze, the bride's and the nun's veil, the frosty shade thanks to which light takes shape and images become perceptible to the ordinary eye: "The screen absorbs and filters the light dimming . . . If words are to be uttered, they would be from behind the partition." The "normal" mind highly distrusts the liquidity of language. Preferring to hold on to what it considers to be clear and solid, it remains necessarily divisive. Cha's artistic, spiritual and survival tools can be partly listed, in her own words, as: "Covering. Draping. Clothing. Sheathe. Shroud./ Superimpose. Overlay. Screen./ Conceal. Ambush./ Disguise. Cache. Mask. Veil./ Obscure. Cloud. Shade. Eclipse. Covert" (Dictée, pp. 131–32).

southern pacific railroad
runs through west

masses china men . . .
each trust of
hammer tearing at
black greased hands body
backs turned to the
mute universe . . .
red agaist the unending[5]
metal   time
          (*Earth*, artist book,
                    1973)

Red and Black: Voices of the Rain

In the whiteness (of metal time), there is black and there is red. *Retour:* a return reveals/re-veils the hues of many other whites—within red, within black. The association of blood, saliva and ink, intensified in French by the resonance between *sang* and *encre* and *sans encre* (without ink), has enjoyed wide currency among writers throughout the times. So does the sound of *cygnes* (swans) and *signes* (signs)—another pairing dear to Cha and to writers for whom water remains a powerful site of dream and memory.

> J'écoutais les cygnes./ Les cygnes dans la pluie. J'écoutais—I heard the swans/ in the rain
> I heard . . . Les signes dans la pluie, j'écoutais./ Les paroles ne sont que pluie devenues neige.—
> The signs in the rain I listened/ the speaking no more than rain having become
> snow.
>
> (*Dictée*, pp. 66–67; 70–71)

Of swans and signs in the rain, of misty and snowy days ("Of white. Mist offers to snow self"), only the images seem to have lasted. On the sheets of time, memory begins charting again and again its eclipses. No end in sight. No ending she can overcome without the actual dying. Listening to the voices of the rain, what she heard, as Cha put it, was—impossible to say—the spoken true or not true in its becoming snow ("her body all the time de composes/ eclipses to be come yours," *Dictée*, p. 118). When she decided to take the Call, all had been rehearsed, and as she seemed to reminisce, the physical impact of what she heard let itself be heard in the Voice (her mother's, her own, Thalia's, Comedy's), which was "Hardly audible at all. Reduced to a moan, a hum, staccato inhalation, and finally a wail." *A Wail.* With no future ahead and "only the onslaught of time," it suddenly seems no longer possible to distinguish with certainty between memory and sign, what was heard, spoken, already said or not said. To prevent the pain from translating itself into memory, "she begins the search the words of equivalence to that of her feeling" (*Dictée*, pp. 139–40). Where to, one may ask, in this return by words? Where else, but in-to the rain (-mist-snow-sheet) that "dreams the sounds" and speaks in more than one language. The cloud-water washes and washes away, not merely to erase, but also to transform the red spilled, which then continues to speak in the darker hue of the Absent: the voice resurrected.

```
snow tides
      white death burying
      the night
      ghost women robed white
      they sing and mourn
      call to the silence remain and fly
                                (Earth)
```

```
into the white they vanish
white where they might impress
a different hue. A shadow
                    (Dictée, p. 128)
```

From behind the cheesecloth partition, one sees the apparition; one hears the shadow-voice by the flickering light of mirrored candles. History is the resurrection "to the very flesh and bone" of the story of division of her ancestry, her people, her native Korea. A history unique to a nation for which "Japan has become the sign. The alphabet. The vocabulary" (Dictée, p. 32). And yet a history whose markings, far from falling prey to the lure of racial exceptionalism (despite the nominal emphasis on "this enemy"), exceed their own specificity to situate themselves within the global conflict of North and South, of the West and the Rest, or of darker and lighter races. No history (of any single nation) without (the) histories (of other nations). Each society has its own politics of truth; each oppressed people, their own story of special horrors and inflicted sufferings. Appeals to a group's victimization, expropriation and dispossession come in more than one color, although the more popularized names remain, predictably enough: occupation, colonization, racism, sexism, homo- and xeno-phobia, planned poverty. The question constantly raised in our times—a time of mass refugeeism, immigration, exile and homelessness; a time when the color line matters—concerns another kind of *twoness*. Not the vertically imposed duality between black and white, nor the mere double consciousness of the oppressed (compelled to weigh one's self by the scale of the oppressor), but the *twohold* (Cha's multilingual hold) of black and red in which infinite shades of white exist. There are, as life dictates, many twos; each equipped with their sets of intervals, recesses and pauses. Many and one between(s). The third term, as I would call it, which keeps the creative potential of a new relationship alive between strategic nationality and transnational political alliance.

Among the atrocities remembered from the times of Japanese occupation, one event stands out in *Dictée* as linked to the name and photo of a young woman: March 1, 1919. Yu Guan Soon: "The eternity of one act." A young revolutionary leader (dead at the age of seventeen) who "will not know age" and will not age: "Child revolutionary child patriot woman soldier deliverer of nation . . . One martyrdom. For the history of one nation. Of one people." Time will stop, especially for some, said Cha—the *diseuse* of her own fortune: "Their countenance evokes not the hallowed beauty, beauty from seasonal decay, evokes not the inevitable, not death, but the dy-ing" (p. 37). So it goes for other sacrificial figures invoked, other photos included, other names, other martyrdom: (Cha's) Mother in her youth, Sister Thérèse, Joan of Arc. *Not death, but the dy-ing*. Swans as well known in literature are an ersatz rather than a mere metaphor of a nude woman. They are equated with the feminine when they are contemplated in pure, luminous waters and with the masculine when they are evoked in their audacious and majestic movements. Swan nudity is highly esteemed for its immaculate and yet ostensible whiteness. Conventional symbolism also tells that the swan's last song before its death, before the supreme moment, is a song of sexual death. Mallarmé, whose life story was marked by the deaths (caused by tuberculosis and chest pains) at a young age, of his mother, then of his sister Maria and his friend Harriet, was known to have cultivated through his work, the power of the poet-medium who wrote at a dead woman's dictation. His poetry abounds with images of apparitions and voices of spectral returns, of She who is departed. It often features the white lily and the red rose in their individualities, and while it affirms "all women are tinted with the blood of roses," what seems to have haunted the poet is the red rose blooming in winter and the white rose turning red in shedding its petals. Dy-ing and resur-recting. *Aller/Retour*, transshaping, fading out and fading in-to color, turning white, turning red, turning black: the thread unfurled in writing goes its own way. In the process of working with the unseen and the Absent, braiding cords while cutting them anew, I come across not only the whites of erasure and departure, but also the whites of beginnings and climaxes—of youth and female martyrdom. As the red of gender absorbs/leaves its imprint on the page screen, the white of virginity and of sexual rite slowly gives off words:

> the memory stain attaches itself and darkens on the pale formless sheet
> . . .
> She opens the cloth again. White. Whitest of beige. In the whiteness,
> subtle hues outlining phoenix from below phoenix from above facing each
> other in the weave barely appearing. Disappearing into the whiteness.
> . . .
> odorless gladiolas white chrysanthemums white
> scents against white sheets to bleed upon
> entwined cloth white heat white mist haze drizzle
> own thickness white liquids to mingle foam retiring
> against pulls prolonging the climax too long
> prepared against the descent too soon to follow.
> Virginity that misses
> virginity consecrated. Already. Elsewhere.
>
> (*Dictée*, pp. 113; 131; 144)

> nirvana
>   this white sheet
>   empty within
>   being middle   balance
> become   in
>   the color word fold
>   paper
>   seed and transmitter
>   without one but all
>
>   (Earth)

Listen to she who sings and mourns with the call of silence. In what language does "white death" speak? In what tongues does the rain dream? In Korean at its bone and flesh levels, in sensual and daunting pouts or in electronic noises mixed with recorded water and bird sounds, one may say looking at *Mouth to Mouth* (video, 1975). Through the camera's "mouth," the viewer is invited to follow its slow pan in close up on the letters of the (English) title, then on some unfamiliar signs—which knowledge reveals to be the eight Korean vowels of Han-gul, formed according to the shape of the mouth as it articulates the sound of the letters. (The return to vernacular sounds and the historical creation of an alphabet accordingly adapted was a necessity shared by East Asian cultures under the hegemony of Chinese language.) Moving on to an empty, highly "pixilated" image, the viewer then sees slowly emerging through the continual vibration of video static a sensual human mouth with parted lips and noticeably white teeth. It opens and closes in slow motion, and when it closes, it barely leaves a trace on the image, remaining visible only through the graphic line of the sealed lips. Image and sound move in slow-paced dissolves—a device explored at length by Cha, a voice or a subject of its own in her visual work. Appearing and disappearing, the mouth performs a number of movements, in which I see, before meaning settles in, a continually shifting play between light and dark shadowy shapes, between concave and convex surfaces, and between static openings and dynamic closures. Sometimes the mouth gaping open would freeze in its movement, leaving the viewer with a strange dark spot on the screen. Despite its immobility, the spot continues to mutate in its visibility; the unfamiliar unexpectedly irrupts into the image and I am no longer sure of what exactly I am seeing: cave, crater, pit—death? (It is here that the piece resonates singularly with Mallarmé's *La Bouche d'ombre*, The Shadow's Mouth or Mouth of the Shades—a voice-resurrection of the past; a shade or shadow that refers not to a "ghost," but to the subtle body of the dead when they appear in front of certain mortals' eyes.) With the repeated re-appearances of the mouth in movement, a link may then be drawn more firmly between the vowels charted at the beginning of the video and the mouth's silent enunciation. The intervals that mark the in-between of the mouth's apparitions are significantly at once loud and silent, busy and empty. Empty and silent, precisely because the sole "content" of these in-between visuals is that which is unique to video (as distinct from film): video static viewed in close up in its restless "snow" motion. Language's liquidity comes to one's ear through the babbling of water punctuated by the chirping of birds, while the dominant sound remains *white noise* (generated with video static) fading in when the mouth fades out.

Speaking Blind through Camera Window

Nothing is stable on the video screen. In its astute use of static and of white noise, *Mouth to Mouth* may be said to feature the video image in its internal structure and unique properties. Just as there is no real movement in film, there is no truly static image in video. One has to produce the effect of a video still the way one produces the illusion of movement through stills in film. With a scanning mechanism that continually etches and erases an image over the screen, video unlike film produces a light of its own, one whose magnetism derives from its continual comings and goings, and its hypnotic vibration. The light box tends to absorb the surrounding space and to draw bystanders' attention through the incessant mutation on screen. With new technology, it promises unending gain in speed, lightness and mobility and has widely become a portable window. It is in this inquiry into the distinctive nature of video and film that one also recognizes in Cha's *Exilée* (film and video installation, 1980).

Using a video monitor embedded into a large film screen, the work is striking for me not so much in its emphatic combination of the two media as in the way the different elements involved play out the relationship between video light and film light. Subtle and rich are the differences made visible in the range of darks and lights, in the minimal and selective contents, in the textures of screen surfaces (curving glass versus white flat wall or partition) and in the exploration of stillness in motion. Here again, time—rather than movement—is shown as being internal to the film image. It is time that one sees unfolding as a plant and its shadow slowly emerge into visibility, as chimerical white curtains blow out of open windows or as light simply travels over a tabletop. And it is time that one hears on video (a medium in which the sense of physical distance and space is largely erased), as the voice-over shuttles between the inside and the outside—evoking inner "exile" in terms of external markers (such as the precise time measurements for the trans-Pacific passage between the United States and Korea).

Although framed by film, video with its black thread (Cha's text on screen) may be said to write the film page, and to stain from within. It dispels in small black letters and leaves—like the pockmarked, floured envelope it shows—its own shape on the white sheet. (Most memorable is, for example, the scene where the video sits in between the two projected windows and curtains of an empty room—a screen within a screen, a window opening onto another window, a box of illusions in an illusory room.) *Exilée*'s (exiled) title, which plays with the French and English spelling of "exile," loses part of itself on screen to become *île* (island), and to end with (one) E, followed by (two) E E—two of the codes that indicate the feminine gender in French grammar. The single and double letters, this feminine of exile(d), ultimately disappear into whiteness. "Twice two times two/ one on top below another one," later says the video voice-over. *There are many twos in the twohold.*

As with Cha's other works, the encounter with her multilingual space of diversified blacks and whites leaves the viewer in a state of subtle suspension—as if transported in mid-flight by a feeling of both undefined loss and utter light/ness. One finds oneself "Awakened in the Mist," *Réveillé dans la brume* (performance, 1977) as she put it, alluding to "'elsewhere' . . . levels in what seems singular in our perception" in her attempt to bring about a transformation on both the receiving and the creating ends. *Rêver* (to dream), *réveil* (waking), re-veils. Floating, bare-foot in measured steps, or so it is said of her, she begins in the darkness, strikes a match, makes light come and go, composing lap dissolve projections while interacting with them, and in the multi-gradations of light, she recites: "everything is light/ everything is dark/ . . . everything feels light/ everything feels dark." *Two times two, twice:* the lifting of the mist and its descent are but the two faces of one reality.

"*Où commencer? début.* debut. fin. end." So begins the voice-over of *Re Dis Appearing* (video, 1977), a work often presented together with *Mouth to Mouth* and *Vidéoème* (video, 1976).

But is it possible at all to speak of a debut, when a disappearance re-appears? Where to start? She asks. Always it seems, by the Two—first *and* last: the swansong of the rain. Some create with the end well in sight ("to write a good novel, you need to have a clear vision of its ending" used to be the advice young writers got from their mentors). Others set out on the journey by letting themselves fall deep into the mist, knowing not where the red cord (string of life, line of creation) leads nor how it will unfold to its end, for there is *no end in sight*. Dy-ing is an eternal end that begins. "We Need a Dead (wo)man to Begin," affirms Hélène Cixous, for whom writing is learning to die: "We must have death, but young, present, ferocious, fresh death, the death of the day, today's death."[6] *Re Dis Appearing* like all of Cha's titles and works, offers multi-leveled perception and reception. With her repeated efforts to unerase while fading out in erasure, to unsay what is said or not yet said and to find the primordial image/sound "before name . . . between name," what comes forth in this re-say (*re-dis*) and re-dis-appearance is: a transparent bowl of tea.

A bowl brought with care into the frame by two hands. As soon as it lands on the glass surface, the bowl doubles and re-doubles—seen with its symmetric reflection, then multiplied via video dissolves and superimposition that surreptitiously alter the look of the object represented. What of this bowl of tea? Water, light, reflection, shadow . . . The opaque transparency. That clear light of death that follows the blackout of consciousness when two bowls come together and separate. Experiences of "doubles," like explorations of memory time, are often as inspiriting as they are unsettling. They can hardly be pinned down or measured, but letting them come, staring at them, invoking, showing and performing them, she does, and does freely—in voided forms and emptied signs: words, sounds, silences, tenses, conjugations, numbers, chronologies and virgin rituals. "The artist's path," as she visualizes it aloud in her work, "is that of a medium" ("Paths," M.F.A. thesis, 1978).

With darkness comes the white light. No matter how dim the sight, a bowl of tea is a de-light. A down-to-earth delight for tea lovers, poor and rich, and an ancient medicine, whose profound healing power is well prized in Asia. To have tea in Buddhist practice is to have a taste of Bodhidharma, for the tale goes that the first tea plant arose from his cut-off eyelids, which fell on the ground. The beverage of awareness keeps one from falling asleep in life as it also induces a state of mind open to nature's gifts. Among the words dropped and woven together around the "tea bowl" in *Re Dis Appearing*, one hears through Cha's voice-over: *le jardin*/ the garden, *thé au sommeil*/ tea of sleep, *les feuilles*/ leaves, *reflété sur l'eau* (reflected in the water), *chaud* (hot), *goût amer* (bitter taste), *déjà passé*/ already passed, a tongue of self.

No, not a tea that induces sleep, but a sleep that provides tea. Always related to the bowl of tea, and always "already passed" is this "tongue of self" that names, bringing into mind a picture of garden, leaves, the reflection in the water and the impression retained by the senses. Bitter, indeed, is the taste of infinity; but bitter also (rather than sweet) are the teas that heal. The two-times-two rhythm goes its way. Doubled and multiplied like the bowl, with one sound slightly delayed in time in relation to the other—as if echoing in both French and English, her voice and its others retains the intense and ethereal quality of dream. As she names, the name appears. The word-image is seen, heard, smelled, tasted and touched.

Death's Voyeur: The All-in-One Diseuse

The tale of Bodhidharma continues its course: the outer eyes must fall off for the inner eye to see. It sees blind and sees into the vast emptiness. She who looks for "the roots of language before it is born on the tip of the tongue" (artist's statement, 1976) has learned the power of writing absent, and speaking silent. In white on black, there where the color is also a non-color, the minimal word-image moves in slow dissolves only to give the impression of transparent immobility. Am I starting a description of *Pause Still* (performance, 1979) or am I referring to *Vidéoème* (video, 1976)? Doesn't the line recall much of the works discussed so far? Does it matter, really, if red is also black when one works with night light? When a body of work crossed media boundaries to find its way into film, video, still photography (slides), performances and handcrafted works (on paper—her artist books—and on fabric)?

All are primarily based on language she said, and language is what defines both the performance and the video. "Opens in black/ closes in black/ closes/ empties itself/ empties itself/ glues itself together and empties again/ . . . at the entry/ the doorway/ the opening/ the closing," she intones in the audio tape of *Pause Still*. Nothing is shown in *Vidéoème* except white letters on black background, in which the play is on the fissures between the seen and heard, and on the wealth of entries in meaning such breaks open onto. Empty the words, empty the silence. Aside from its deconstruction of the title— into emptied (*vidé*), empty, emptiness (*vide*), a single O (and its rich symbolism) as linked to *vide*, and to *ème* as with *poème*, a video-poem, or to (i) *ème*, an nth of video (*vidéoème*)—the piece offers an almost literal realization of the Zen hearing eye and speaking ear by showing "sound" while saying "see" and thus goes the pair of visual and audio tracks: "empty-see;" "to see-empty;" "emptied-to see."

Seeing absent, speaking blind. In an earlier performance, Cha is already seen with a headband marked *Voix* (voice) tied over her eyes and another marked *Aveugle* (blind) tied over her mouth while unrolling a white banner with letters written on it that read: *aveugle/ voix/ sans/ mot/ sans/ me* (*Aveugle Voix*, performance, 1975). Worth noting is not so much the designation and combination of Blind and Voice as the resonance of these words when they are taken in reverse order: *Aveugle Voix*, rather than the usual, grammatically correct, *Voix Aveugle*. By making the reading of both possible (through the position of these words on the headbands and on the banner), she introduces the eye that hears into the space of blind voice—without word (*sans mot*), without me (*sans me*). The play on *voix* (voice) and *voir* (to see) is all the more significant for without seeing the written letters, *Aveugle Voix* and (l') *aveugle voit* (the blind sees) sound the same.

Much has been written on the voice of *Dictée* as related to the fragmented process of coming to speech, to the difficulty of articulating within the bounds of the Master's language, as well as to the loss of one's mother tongue in the context of colonization and immigration. And, for those who have known the bitter taste of French education, the lesson of grammar and dictation remains undeniably *the* nightmare that spares no one—foreigners and natives alike, including the philosopher Jean-Paul Sartre who, as a child prodigy, found himself dropped to the lowest level after he turned in his dictation assignment in which he wrote: "*le lapen çovache ême le ten*" (*le lapin sauvage aime le thym*).[7] The voice presented in *Dictée* is thus mainly depicted as stuttering, failing in its mimicking

from Night Passage

and being suppressed in its fragmentation and interruptions. However, listening to Cha's voice in her visual works leaves one with a considerably different feeling, as it leads one, by her words, to (an) "elsewhere level(s) in what seems singular in our perception."

Slowly repeats, slowly modifies itself, slowly disintegrates and then, slowly begins anew. Multiplication of periods and pauses. Words decomposed, repeated, sometimes misspelled, sometimes mispronounced, isolated and incomplete. If failure there is, then it is a failure à la Beckett (fail again, fail better)—a failure that retains its agency in a supposedly non-failing, successful society. If it stutters, then *Worstward Ho* also stutters (although Beckett does not truly hesitate and his silences are not "tea silence"), for contemporary French writers and philosophers love to depict their searching activities and their best writings as "*bégaiement*" (a stuttering). The line between the mis-spelled, the un-spelled and the re-spelled is tenuous. After all, the writing of *Dictée* is also a writing *dictated* by at least nine muses. Cha's voice appears to me, in all its pauses and lapses, primarily as a voice that remains attentive to the single sound of the word and to its physical impact. A voice that serves as a site for rich resonance and metamorphoses generated in the endless possible combinations that language offers.

The ability to suspend the tone of a voice or of writing, and to hear its resonance while it is being produced is a skill difficult to acquire when one writes and speaks without listening absent, to one's own speech. The written word that hears and the spoken word that sees its sound are disquieting, for what they let see and hear is the silence and the infinitely more of speech and language. Death irrupting into and in between the words. Marguerite Duras, who has radically expanded the Voice in cinema, is said to have given birth in her writing to "a strange speech: speech which moves in that inner zones of silence where the power of hearing is spoken."[8] The voice-over of *Exilée* (whose tone remains distinct from *Re Dis Appearing*, for example) particularly reminds me of the echoing voices in Duras' *India Song*, which carry single words and fragments of sentences without a definite subject or object. It is this captivating power of a spoken ear that one recognizes in Cha's voice, across her books and visual work. Hers is a voice in which the work of dream and of night survives.

> The violence of poetry
>   is still
>   and goes deep—
>   to the bone
>   to the white
>   (Kenneth White,
>   *The Bird Path*)[9]

In dream, the unfinished returns again and again, each time with fresh intensity. No end in sight. "I" fare without the certainty of "me" and the other "s/he" shuttles in more than one body even while remaining whom I think s/he is. Every figure that appears in the dream seems to pass onto another one and onto yet another, indefinitely. The one whom I seem to have unquestioningly recognized through more than one appearance becomes unidentifiable upon waking, for the one-many has simply turned into the many. In *Dictée*, the chapter "Erato/Love Poetry" which opens with a photo of St Thérèse is significantly written as a film script.

> She is entering now . . . She enters the screen from the left, before the titles fading in and out . . . She takes the fourth seat from the left. The utmost center of the room . . . She is drawn to the white, then the black. In the whiteness the shadows move across, dark shapes and dark light.
>
> (p. 94)

The entire focus is accordingly on what can be "objectively" *seen from the outside.* Directions are further given for the camera shots in the scenes composed. The reader is thus told what to see from a camera's point of view as it frames the movements of an indefinite "she." With Theresa dangerously looking at (St) Thérèse the call for both distance and identification is inevitable. She is here at once the one who looks and the one looked at—inside the screen and watching it; spectator and actor; audience and performer; writer and written: "i am the object/ you are the subject . . . you are the object/ i am the subject . . ." (*Audience Distance Relative*, artist book, 1977). Two times two, twofold, she says, two holds.

> —Where is woman in this film (*India Song*)? (X. Gauthier)
> — In the one who dies. (M. Duras)[10]

Without her seeing absent, the space of memory and autobiography could hardly be the site where the historical, the personal, the mythical and the spiritual meet so intricately. Some of the most emotionally intense and moving passages of *Dictée* are precisely those in which what seems to stand closest to Cha's heart—her mother and father—is seen through the camera's eye in terms of an emblematic relationship between husband and wife. In a previous chapter, "Calliope/Epic Poetry," which opens with a photo of Cha's mother in her youth, Cha chooses an apparently direct mode of address: "mother, you" to narrate her life. Yet, the addressee is not quite the mother (who needs not be told in details about her own past). By the specifics given in the telling, she is only present through her absence, and it is the third and second absent presences of the writer and reader that make themselves felt through the narration. The addressee is inscribed as a plural in the text, and Mother is not merely to be found there where she is explicitly located—in time, place, and movement. Letting Mother come to memory, letting "she" surface as multiplicity, speaking blind to her image as to oneself in display . . . I to I, she of she. With such a direct-in-the-indirect "you," writing's demand utterly occupies the central seat.

As Cha moves to the more indirect and impersonal "she," Mother becomes even more expansive for she is at once mother, her mother, her daughter and the latter's same-others. Looking through the camera at Her, her sorrow and her endurance, is looking at the condition of a whole generation of Asian women in their relation to silence and language. In dealing with the intimate and the autobiographical, Cha does not need to claim the insider's position of truth, for she is She. *Seed and transmitter/ without* one but all (Earth). Rather than making use of the internal psychological voice that remains the norm in autobiographical narratives, Cha looks at her mother/herself from the outside— the way a camera gazes at its subject. Pain and suffering are evoked only through what the camera can catch as displayed in a mise-en-scène. The rigor of such work of exteriority in writing and the near-distance effect heightens rather than diminishes the emotional impact, for it is a(n Audience) Distance Relative—intimate, intense and yet not sentimental.

> She says to herself she could displace real time. She says to herself she could display it before and become its voyeur . . . *She says to herself if she were able to write she could continue to live . . . To herself if by writing she could abolish real time. She would live. If she could display it before her and become its voyeur . . .*
>
> Let the one who is *diseuse,* one who is mother, who waits nine days and nine nights be found. *Restore memory. Let the one who is diseuse, one who is daughter restore spring with her each appearance from beneath the earth.*
>
> *The ink spills thickest before it runs dry before it stops writing at all.*
>
> (Dictée, pp. 140–41; 133)

Dreamer and dream, medium, alchemist, magician, fortune-story-teller. She is the all-in-one *diseuse* who, in mirth and in mist, warns against the danger of letting language fall into disuse. To her, return *never-ending,* these words of flesh and bone heard in their very earth tone:

> when spring come
> forgotten flowers
> fill   awaken
> the bare winter
> fold back the snow
> to hear green shoots
> small streams
>   (Earth)

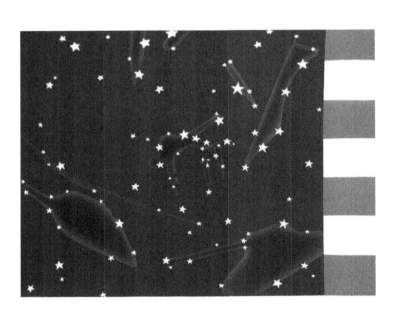

Detroit

Incarcerated and Disappeared in the Land of the Free

Speech delivered at "The Crisis in Urban America" Educational Summit, August 20, 2002, Detroit, Michigan.

There has been a time in the sixties, for example, when revolutionary leadership can with good conscience endeavor to open people's eyes and cure them from their blindness. But, today when opposites meet in the same rhetoric of Good and Evil, and bringing the invisible into visibility is no longer a simple one-way task, it seems more adequate to acknowledge that one is often blind, even with one's eyes open—until one learns to see, even with eyes wide shut.

Illiteracy, incarceration, segregation, unemployment, poverty, homicide and infanticide, as well as misogyny, rape and child abuse. The multifaceted problems we encountered in urban centers across the nation tell us with poignancy something about ourselves, about the system in which we participate, and about the irrevocable process of globalization. It is no accident that America with its incarceration rate has also proven to be the world's most aggressive jailer. And, it is no accident that Detroit, one of the ten largest cities in the nation, a city well known for its sustained protests and rebellions in the forties and sixties, should also be among those struggling the hardest with illiteracy and unemployment. In a context where almost 70 percent of Metro Detroit students attend schools that are either 90 percent black or 90 percent white, one cannot help but notice how external and internal divisions of the State and the cities pass into one another in mutual reflection and reiteration.

We live with the remnants of a mind-set fixed on material evidence and accumulation, and on social structures built to separate, divide and conquer. With this in mind, it is hardly surprising that an educational system functioning as the pillar of these structures should become the enemy of certain youth groups; and literacy, no more no less than a means to maintain them in line and promote conformity. As we face today's complex world networks of communication and dis-information in which logic is processed and language computerized, we are bound at times to question the validity of literacy—the assimilation into a dehumanizing machine so impoverished in spirit and imagination as to promote profit as the sole measure of value and economic growth as the sole measure of progress. Advanced technology can turn many of us, literate, into refugees; it can program us into conformity to the logic of a war machine that places numbers, quotas and the market well above the person.

Disfranchised groups continued to be treated as irregular cases—in which are marginal, abnormal and "other" all those individuals who deviate from the norms of a "good" and "just" society. As proven by practices fed into and disseminated by the media, these individuals are primarily (news) items; items to be quoted, traded and exploited in the system of commodified diversity. They are, by the same token, easily lumped together when the need to give a face to an invisible culprit calls for specific strategies of profiling. The targeting of neighborhoods, for example, feeds on the logic that "They are all criminals who *look like* one" and *live there* where a greater crime rate is to be found. What is generated from inside the very core of a structure is deceptively isolated, displaced as outside society and dealt with as an alien element that needs conversion in order to be integrated. Evil is presented as coming from elsewhere and all that are needed to make it disappear is a precise cosmetic surgery with advanced technology. So goes the logic, and surely enough, what applies on the local and national scale inevitably applies on the global scale with U.S. foreign policy and warfare.

The dynamics of multiculturalism is world mediated. The war on terrorism has crystallized many of our phobias and prejudices. It gives racial profiling a new twist, while highlighting issues of immigration, identification, nationalization, as well as cultural and gender discrimination. There is a link between the way we define our elusive enemy abroad and the way we deal with our "others" at home, and certainly, there is a deep link between the way we identify our enemy and the way we define ourselves. We are being called upon to believe that we can eradicate terrorism by detaining and cross-examining outsiders in our midst. Such an attempt to define who's inside and who's outside in a society as heterogeneous as ours not only widens the divide between Americans and the world, the West and the Rest, but it also shows further conflicts among the multiply diverse fractions of our society. It has led to what a number of lawyers across the nation see as a dramatic constitutional crisis in U.S. history.

Blanket detentions, random searches, racial profiling and arbitrary prosecution of those who look suspect to our eyes, are some of the solutions that have been adopted to give a visible front to what terrifies us. The enemy here is likely to be anyone who triggers the deep layers of our fear for the unexpected, the unknown, the abnormal, the foreign, in short, otherness as death. Each apparatus creates its own antibodies and its own enemies from within, and if blackness is equated with destruction in Detroit, on the world map, Africa is associated with AIDS, South America with drugs, Islam with terrorism, and the Third World with debt. The application of different standards to different people, the attack on suspicious-looking members of our society, their secret and indefinite confinement have led to an oddly regressive social phenomenon: that of the disappeared in the land of the free.

An eye for an eye and the world goes blind, as peace activists have reminded us. Behind the appearance of socialization, integration and participation, policies are set up that de-socialize, disenfranchise and alienate whole communities. Sophisticated technology, clever economic exchange and exploitation (corporate robbery in our country, deceptive foreign aid, investment and free trade in the Third World are a few examples among many) dominate the social order, turning other sectors into dumping grounds or deserted zones for the poor and the rebel. With this in mind, the urgent task, as I see it, would be to bring to continual practice the critical role of civil society in "democratizing democracy."

For educators like ourselves, such a commitment to freedom rather than to domination and submission in education would entail a constant questioning of our relationship to knowledge, to the way we reserve, transmit or bring it to bear on our daily activities. Our ongoing critical view of the system is motivated, not by a mere desire to blame, to right the wrongs and to oppose for opposition's sake. Rather, it is motivated by the necessity to keep power and knowledge (ours and theirs) constantly in check for our own survival. Considering the struggle that women of such groups as the So Sad in Detroit have been carrying on against child homicide and violent crime, the recent agreement of the Justice Department and Detroit to call in a monitor to oversee reform at the Police Department after years of complaints of misconduct is, hopefully, not a small step up in critical intervention and joint responsibility for social change. As a woman from an office of Save Our Sons and Daughters in the city put it, "We had 9/11 before 9/11 . . . We have it going on every day."

To say this, however, is also to say that the times of great difficulties are also the most enriching times. Ours is a time of change, of learning, of gaining wisdom and internal strength. A time when educators, artists, activists and other path makers are reminded that color, class, gender and culture are not categories, but an ongoing project and a dimension of consciousness. The capacity to transform ourselves and others in the very instance of our daily performances lies in the ability to expand our views and to create new, unexpected relationships among things, events and people. An educational praxis committed to changes in both the literate and the illiterate spheres should, among others, offer the possibility of a radical self-awareness in which words, language are not just an exercise of power or resistance but also an infinite act of creativity.

(August 20, 2002, Detroit, Michigan)

Notes

Foreignness and the New Color of Fear

1 Inayat Khan, *Music* (Claremont, California: Hunter House Inc., 1959, rpt. 1962, 1988), p. 16.
2 Quoted in Zaha Hassan & Steven Goldberg—National Lawyers Guild, "Israel's Wall: An Analysis of Its Legal Validity Under U.S. and International Law," http://www.endtheoccupation.org/article.php?list=type&type=68.
3 Carol Chehade, "Arabs and the Racial Lessons of 9/11," SeeingBlack.com, February 28, 2003, http://seeingblack.com/2003/x022803/arabs.shtml.

Far Away, From Home: The Comma Between

1 Trinh T. Minh-ha, *When the Moon Waxes Red: Representation, Gender and Cultural Politics* (New York & London: Routledge, 1991), pp. 81–105.
2 Quoted by memory. My italics.

Other Than Myself, My Other Self

1 Tahar Ben Jelloun, "Les Pierres du temps," *Traverses*, No. 40 (1987), p. 158. Unless indicated otherwise, all translations from the French are mine.
2 Gary Snyder, *The Practice of the Wild* (San Francisco: Northpoint Press, 1990), p. 7.
3 Jelloun, "Les Pierres du temps," p. 159.
4 Tahar Ben Jelloun, *Moha le fou, Moha le sage* (Paris: Seuil, 1978), p. 10.
5 Maurice Blanchot, *Vicious Circles*, trans. P. Auster (Barrytown, New York: Station Hill Press, 1985), p. 19.
6 Edward Said, "Reflections on Exile," in *Out There: Marginalization and Contemporary Culture*, eds. R. Fergusson et al. (New York: The New Museum of Contemporary Art and M.I.T. Press, 1990), pp. 357–58.
7 Quoted in Bruce Grant et al., *The Boat People: An "Age" Investigation* (New York: Penguin Books, 1979), p. 182.
8 Quoted in ibid., p. 173.
9 Ibid., p. 195.

10 Terms used by a Halifax woman with regards to Canada and the flux of South East-Asian refugees in the late seventies, reported in ibid., p. 174.

11 Blanchot, *Vicious Circles*, p. 66.

12 Julia Kristeva, in *The Kristeva Reader*, ed. T. Moi (New York: Columbia University Press, 1986), pp. 298; 296. Original italics.

13 Ibid., p. 286.

14 Quoted in Hannah Arendt's introduction, in Walter Benjamin, *Illuminations* (New York: Schocken Books, 1969), p. 20.

15 Said, "Reflections on Exile," p. 357.

16 Ibid., pp. 364–65. Original italics.

17 Snyder, *The Practice of the Wild*, pp. 23–24.

18 Edward Said, "The Voice of a Palestinian in Exile," in *Third Text*, Nos. 3/4 (Spring–Summer, 1988), p. 48.

19 All quoted in Lucy R. Lippard, *Mixed Blessings: New Art in a Multicultural America* (New York: Pantheon, 1990), pp. 23; 30; 170; 47; 41; 151.

20 Benjamin, *Illuminations*, p. 73.

21 Pham Van Ky, *Des Femmes assises çà et là* (Paris: Gallimard, 1964), pp. 8; 18. The quoted passage was translated in J. A. Yeager, *The Vietnamese Novel in French: A Literary Response to Colonialism* (Hanover: University Press of New England, 1986), pp. 151–52.

22 Elaine K. Chang, "A Not-So-New Spelling of My Name: Notes Toward (and Against) a Politics of Equivocation," in *Displacement: Cultural Identities in Question*, ed. Angelika Bammer (Bloomington: Indiana University Press, 1994).

23 See, for example, the articles published in *Traverses*, Nos. 41–42 (issue on "Voyages", 1987), more particularly those written by J.-C. Guillebaud, J.-D. Urbain, P. Curvel, P. Virilio, V. Vadsarid, P. Sansot, C. Wulf, F. Affergan and C. Reichler.

24 See J. Culler, "Semiotics of Tourism," *American Journal of Semiotics*, Nos. 1–2 (1981), p. 130.

25 Jean-Didier Urbain, "Le Voyageur detrousse," *Traverses*, Nos. 41–42 (1987), pp. 43; 48.

26 Benjamin, *Illuminations*, p. 81.

27 Christoph Wulf, "La Voie lactée," *Traverses*, Nos. 41–42 (1987), p. 128.

28 Marguerite Duras, as interviewed by Xavière Gauthier in *Les Parleuses* (Paris: Minuit, 1974), pp. 11–12.

29 Marguerite Duras, in *New French Feminisms: An Anthology*, eds. E. Marks & I. de Courtivron (Amherst: The University of Massachusetts Press, 1980), pp. 111–12.

30 Jean-Claude Guillebaud, "Une Ruse de la littérature," *Traverses*, Nos. 41–42 (1987), p. 16.

An Acoustic Journey

1 Jean Genet, *Prisoner of Love*, trans. B. Bray (Hanover, New Hampton & London: Wesleyan University Press, 1992), p. 12.

2 Comment on the Vietnamese camps by Chuman, RAFU Shimpo, May 21, 1975. Quoted by William T. Liu et al., *Transition to Nowhere: Vietnamese Refugees in America* (Nashville, Tennessee: Charter House Publishers Inc., 1979), p. 102.

3 Barry Wain, *The Refused: The Agony of the Indochina Refugees* (New York: Simon and Schuster, 1981), p. 10. My italics.

4 See E. F. Kunz, "The Refugee in Flight: Kinetic Models and Forms of Displacement," *International Migration Review*, No. 7 (1973), pp. 125–46.

5 Nguyen Thi Trau, quoted in Liu et al., *Transition to Nowhere*, p. 170.

6 Gloria Anzaldúa, *Borderlands/La Frontera: The New Mestiza* (San Francisco: Aunt Lute Books, 1987), p. 194.

7 Stuart Hall, "New Ethnicities," *Black Film, British Cinema (ICA Documents)*, No. 7 (London: Institute of Contemporary Arts, 1988), p. 28.

8 Henri Louis Gates, Jr., *Loose Canons* (New York: Oxford University Press, 1992), p. 183.

9 Ibid., p. 185.

10 Genet, *Prisoner of Love*, pp. 47; 83–84; 86.

11 Ibid., p. 218.

12 See Martin Luther King, Jr., *Where Do We Go From Here: Chaos or Community?* (New York: Bantam Books, 1968).

13 Genet, *Prisoner of Love*, p. 42.

14 Ibid., pp. 258; 148.

15 Ibid., p. 149. My italics.

16 Ibid., p. 7.

17 King, *Where Do We Go From Here . . .?*, p. 43.

18 Genet, *Prisoner of Love*, pp. 318–19.

19 In *Making Face, Making Soul/Haciendo Caras*, ed. Gloria Anzaldúa (San Francisco: Aunt Lute Foundation Books, 1990), pp. 300–301.

20 Anzaldúa, *Borderlands/La Frontera*, p. 20.

21 Ibid., p. 21.

22 Ibid., pp. 83; 77.

23 June Jordan, "Where Is the Love?," in Anzaldúa, *Making Face, Making Soul*, p. 174.

24 Audre Lorde, "I Am Your Sister: Black Women Organizing Across Sexualities," in Anzaldúa, *Making Face, Making Soul*, pp. 321; 325. Original italics.

25 Herbert Marcuse, *Counter-revolution and Revolt* (Boston: Beacon Press, 1972), p. 74.

26 John Cage, *Silence* (Middletown, Connecticut: Wesleyan University Press, 1961), p. x.

27 Matsuo Basho, quoted in *Sources of Japanese Tradition*, eds. Ryusaku Tsunoda et al. (New York: Columbia University Press, 1958, rpt. 1965), p. 456.

Nature's r: A Musical Swoon

All translations from the French are mine, unless otherwise indicated.

1 Quoted from memory.

2 Jean Baudrillard, "The Anorexic Ruins," in *Looking Back on the End of the World*, ed. D. Kamper & C. Wulf, trans. D. Antal (New York: Semiotext(e), 1989), p. 45.

3 Simone de Beauvoir, *The Second Sex*, trans. H. M. Parshley (New York: Bantam, 1952), p. 669.

4 Baudrillard, "The Anorexic Ruins," p. 45.

5 Cheikh Amidou Kane, *Ambiguous Adventure*, trans. K. Woods (New York: Walker & Company, 1963), pp. 75–80.

6 Boubou Hama, *Le Double d'hier rencontre demain* (Paris: Union Générale d'Edition, 1973), p. 29.

7 Peter Kubelka, "The Theory of Metrical Film," in *The Avant-Garde Film: A Reader of Theory and Criticism*, ed. P. A. Sitney (New York: Anthology Film Archives, 1987), p. 158.

8 Jean-Joseph Rabearivelo, "Le vitrier nègre," in A. Grard, *Etudes de littérature africaine francophone* (Dakar: Les Nouvelles Editions Africaines, 1977), p. 83.

9 Kane, *Ambiguous Adventure*, p. 48.

10 A. Hampâté Ba, *Kaydara* (Dakar: Les Nouvelles Editions Africaines, 1978), p. 10.

11 M. R. James, as quoted in Edward Wagenknecht, *Seven Masters of Supernatural Fiction* (New York: Greenwood Press, 1991), p. 51.

12 Anthony Vidler, *The Architectural Uncanny* (Cambridge, Massachusetts: The M.I.T. Press, 1992), p. 17.

13 Claude Lévi-Strauss, *Structural Anthropology*, Vol. II, trans. M. Layton (New York: Basic Books Inc., 1976), p. 320.

14 As quoted in Wagenknecht, *Seven Masters of Supernatural Fiction*, p. 71.

15 Hama, *Le Double d'hier rencontre demain*, p. 409, footnote 4.

16 Hampâté Ba, *Kaydara*, p. 83.

17 Hama, *Le Double d'hier rencontre demain*, p. 203.

18 John Cage, *Pour les oiseaux* (Paris: Pierre Belfond, 1976), p. 231.

19 Ananda K. Coomaraswamy, *The Transformation of Nature in Art* (New York: Dover Publications, 1934), p. 11.

20 Ibid., pp. 128; 129. My italics.

21 R. G. H. Siu, *The Tao of Science* (Cambridge, Massachusetts: The M.I.T. Press, 1957), p. 78.

22 Ibid., p. 76.

23 In François Cheng, *Souffle-esprit* (Paris: Les Editions du Seuil, 1989), pp. 33–34. My translation.

24 In ibid., p. 56.

25 In ibid., pp. 114–15.

26 Quoted in Coomaraswamy, *The Transformation of Nature in Art*, p. 15.

27 In Cheng, *Souffle-esprit*, pp. 30; 46–47.

28 Gilles Deleuze & Felix Guattari, *A Thousand Plateaus*, trans. B. Massumi (Minneapolis: University of Minnesota Press, 1987), p. 25. My italics.

29 Ibid., p. 305.

30 Ibid., p. 25.

31 Siu, *The Tao of Science*, p. 127.

32 Deleuze & Guattari, *A Thousand Plateaus*, p. 25.

33 See Toshihiko Izutsu, "The Elimination of Colour in Far Eastern Art and Philosophy," in *Color Symbolism* (Dallas, Texas: Spring Publications Inc., 1977), pp. 185–89.

34 Siu, *The Tao of Science*, p. 71.

35 Ooka Makoto, *The Colors of Poetry: Essays in Classic Japanese Verse*, trans. Takato U. Lento & Thomas V. Lento (Rochester, Michigan: Katydid Books, 1991), pp. 37; 39.

36 Quoted in Izutsu, "The Elimination of Colour in Far Eastern Art and Philosophy," p. 176.

37 Ibid., pp. 168–69.

38 Information largely given in ibid., pp. 170–74.

39 Kisho Kurokawa, *Rediscovering Japanese Space* (New York: Weatherhill, 1988), p. 405. Previous information on Rikyu gray is largely taken from ibid., pp. 53–70. See also Kurokawa's *Intercultural Architecture: The Philosophy of Symbiosis* (Washington, DC: The American Institute of Architects Press, 1991).

40 Kurokawa, *Rediscovering Japanese Space*, p. 58.

41 Kurokawa, *Intercultural Architecture*, p. 70.

42 Roger Garaudy, quoted in Maria Mies & Vandana Shiva, *Ecofeminism* (London: Zed Books, 1993), p. 137.

43 Information gathered in J. Chevalier & A. Gheerbrant, *Dictionnaire des symboles* (Paris: Editions R. Laffont & Editions Jupiter, 1969).

44 John Hedgecoe, *The Art of Color Photography* (New York: Simon and Schuster, 1978), p. 126.

45 Jean Genet, *Prisoner of Love*, trans. B. Bray (Hanover, New Hampton & London: Wesleyan University Press, 1992), p. 220.

46 Ibid., p. 221.

The Paint of Music

1 Zeami, "The Book of the Way of the Highest Flower (Shikado-sho)," in *Sources of Japanese Tradition*, eds. R. Tsunoda, W. T. de Bary & D. Keene (New York: Columbia University Press, 1958, rpt. 1965), p. 301.

2 Ibid., pp. 302–303.

3 A statement inspired by the writings of Kukai. Matsuo Basho, "The Rustic Gate," in *Sources of Japanese Tradition*, eds. Tsunoda, de Bary & Keene, p. 459.

4 Jerzy Grotowski, quoted in Zbigniew Osinski, "Grotowski Blazes the Trails: From Objective Drama to Ritual Arts," *The Drama Review* (TDR), Vol. 35, No. 1 (Spring, 1991), p. 106.

5 Basho, quoted in Makoto Ueda, *Matsuo Basho* (Japan: Kodansha International Ltd., 1970, rpt. 1982), p. 163.

6 Basho, "The Rustic Gate," p. 458.

7 See Daisetz T. Suzuki, *Zen and Japanese Culture* (Princeton, New Jersey: Princeton University Press, 1970, rpt. 1973), pp. 224–25.

8 Roland Barthes, *Empire of Signs*, trans. R. Howard (New York: Hill & Wang, 1982), pp. 69; 76.

9 Suzuki, *Zen and Japanese Culture*, p. 228.

10 Merce Cunningham, quoted in Susan Leigh Foster, *Reading Dancing: Bodies and Subjects in Contemporary American Dance* (Berkeley: University of California Press, 1986), pp. 35–36. Previous quotes in this paragraph are also Cunningham's own words. For a more comprehensive analysis of his dances, see ibid., chapter 1, pp. 1–57.

11 Quoted in *Sources of Japanese Tradition*, eds. Tsunoda, de Bary & Keene, p. 284.

12 Ibid., p. 291.

13 Nishida Kitaro, quoted in Earle J. Coleman, *Philosophy of Painting by Shih T'ao* (New York: Mouton Publishers, 1978), p. 13.

14 Shin'ichi Hisamatsu, as quoted in Coleman, *Philosophy of Painting by Shih T'ao*, p. 15.

15 Zeami, quoted in Kisho Kurokawa, *Rediscovering Japanese Space* (New York: Weatherhill, 1988), p. 66.

16 Inayat Khan, *Music* (Claremont, California: Hunter House Inc., 1988), p. 13.

17 See ibid., pp. 33–35.

18 Quoted in Richard Trousdell, "Peter Sellars Rehearses Figaro," TDR, Vol. 35, No. 1 (Spring, 1991), p. 71.

19 Marguerite Duras, "Smothered Creativity," in *New French Feminisms: An Anthology*, eds. E. Marks & I. de Courtivron (Amherst: University of Massachusetts Press, 1980), p. 111.

20 Marguerite Duras, "From An Interview," in ibid., pp. 174–75.

21 Pierre Félida, "Between the Voices and the Images," in Marguerite Duras, *Duras by Duras* (San Francisco: City Lights Books, 1987), pp. 147–48. Original italics.

22 Mickey Hart, *Drumming at the Edge of Magic: A Journey into the Spirit of Percussion* (San Francisco: HarperCollins, 1990), p. 12.

23 From "An Act Against All Power," an interview with Marguerite Duras by J. Grant & J. Frenais, in Duras, *Duras by Duras*, p. 120.

24 Dionys Mascolo, "Birth of Tragedy," in ibid., p. 135.

25 Roland Barthes, *The Responsibility of Forms: Critical Essays on Music, Art, and Representation*, trans. R. Howard (New York: Hill & Wang, 1985), p. 124.

26 Robert Bresson, *Notes sur le cinématographe* (Paris: Gallimard, 1975), p. 123. My translation and italics.

27 Basho, "The Rustic Gate," p. 458.

28 Julia Kristeva, "Ces Femmes au-delà du plaisir," *Art Press*, Hors Série No. 4 (December 1984–January 1985), p. 31. For previous quotes from Godard, see Jean-Luc Godard, "La Curiosité du sujet," *Art Press*, Hors Série No. 4 (December 1984–January 1985), pp. 12–16.

29 Bernard Dufour, "Les Peintures et Godard," *Art Press*, Hors Série No. 4 (December 1984–January 1985), pp. 59–61. The "Beethoven" label mentioned earlier is by Jacques Drillon, ibid., p. 62.

30 Bresson, *Notes sur le cinématographe*, p. 128.

31 Quoted on back cover of the above issue of *Art Press*.

Mother's Talk

1 "Maman-caiman," in Birago Diop, *Les Contes d'Amadou Koumba* (Paris: Présence africaine, 1961), pp. 49–57. Translations from the French are largely taken from the English version "Mother Crocodile," in *Tales of Amadou Koumba*, trans. Dorothy S. Blair (London: Oxford University Press, 1966), pp. 45–51.

2 Mohamadou Kane, *Birago Diop: L'Homme et l'oeuvre* (Paris: Présence africaine, 1971), p. 37. My translation.

3 Roger D. Abrahams, *African Folktales* (New York: Pantheon, 1983), p. 22.

4 Diop, *Les Contes d'Amadou Koumba*, p. 47.

5 Quoted as a representative statement of the African conception of the supernatural in Kane, *Birago Diop*, p. 68.

6 In Alta Jablow, *Yes and No: The Intimate Folklore of Africa* (New York: Horizon Press, 1961), p. 127.

7 In Henri Gaden, *Proverbes et maximes peuls et toucouleurs* (Paris: Institut d'ethnologie, 1931), pp. 15–16. My translations.

8 Collected in René Luneau, *Chants de femmes au Mali* (Paris: Luneau Ascot Éditeurs, 1981), p. 156. My translation.

9 In Gaden, *Proverbes et maximes peuls et toucouleurs*, p. 148.

10 Quoted in Andrey Tarkovsky, *Sculpting in Time: Reflections on the Cinema*, trans. K. Hunter-Blair (New York: Alfred A. Knopf, 1987), p. 116.

White Spring

1 Theresa Hak Kyung Cha, unpublished description of *A Ble Wail*, performance at the Worth Ryder Gallery, University of California at Berkeley, 1975. All of the documents and works by Cha discussed here are available at Berkeley Art Museum and Pacific Film Archive, University of California, Berkeley.

2 Theresa Hak Kyung Cha, *Dictée* (New York: Tanam Press, 1982; rpt Berkeley: Third Woman Press, 1995). Hereon indicated in my text only by its title followed by the page number.

3 Marguerite Duras, *Practicalities*, trans. B. Bray (New York: Grove Weidenfeld, 1990), p. 25.

4 In *Apparatus*, ed. Theresa Hak Kyung Cha (New York: Tanam Press, 1980).

5 Spelling as is.

6 Hélène Cixous, *Three Steps on the Ladder of Writing*, trans. S. Cornell & S. Sellers (New York: Columbia University Press, 1993), p. 7.

7 Jean-Paul Sartre, *The Words*, trans. B. Frechtman (New York: George Braziller, 1964), p. 77.

8 Pierre Félida, "Between the Voices and the Image," in Marguerite Duras, *Duras by Duras* (San Francisco: City Lights Books, 1987), p. 147.

9 Kenneth White, *The Bird Path* (Edinburgh: Mainstream Publishing, 1989), p. 96.

10 From "Dispossessed," an interview with Marguerite Duras by X. Gauthier, in Duras, *Duras by Duras*, p. 77.

Index

Note: alphabetical arrangement is letter-by-letter.

#0211 - 220917 - C0 - 254/178/9 - PB - 9780415880220